Understanding What Matters Most

THE BOOK OF Ecclesiastes

Understanding What Matters Most

THE BOOK OF Ecclesiastes

STEPHANIE SHOTT

God's Word to you is our highest calling.

Following God

THE BOOK OF ECCLESIASTES: UNDERSTANDING WHAT MATTERS MOST

First Printing, 2011

ISBN: 978-0-89957-024-2

Editing by Rich Cairnes, Rick Steele, and Dr. Warren Baker
Layout by Jennifer Ross and Rick Steele
Cover design by Michael Largent at Indoor Graphics, Chattanooga, Tennessee

Printed in the United States of America
16 15 14 13 12 11 –CH– 6 5 4 3 2 1

Acknowledgments

I love knowing so many hands and hearts have gone into writing this Bible study!

Certainly, Jesus gets the biggest "Thank You" human words could possibly express. He truly does exceedingly, abundantly above all we could ask or think!

A very special thanks to my ever-patient and always-encouraging husband, Donald. He has loved me enough to pray some crazy, audacious prayers for me and he has believed in me even when I didn't believe in myself.

I'm also grateful to my sons, Karl and D.J., who unknowingly inspire me with their wit and creativity.

I owe a great debt of gratitude to the late Dan Penwell whose "yes" expanded my ministry borders beyond my wildest dreams. And much thanks goes to Rick Steele, who has patiently walked this newbie author through her first steps in the publishing world. Special thanks to Warren Baker for the necessary prepress work and for making the final corrections.

Author Rick Shepherd and his wife, Linda Gail, challenge me with their consistently relentless pursuit to impact this world for Christ. Dawn Bryant has been that Proverbs 17:17 friend. Examples from her life are sprinkled throughout this book. And finally, thank you to Susie Reinhardt and Marsha Spicer for loving me enough to read through my manuscript when it was still raw and then helping me think beyond myself.

"Two are better than one, because they have a good [more satisfying] reward for their labor." (Ecclesiastes 4:9, Amplified Bible)

Stephanie Shott

About the Author

Stephanie Shott knows her life was divinely interrupted and her heart radically transformed by the Living God in 1987. Since that time, the Lord has allowed her to serve as a Bible teacher and conference speaker to women of all ages and gave her the privilege of serving Him as a missionary to Costa Rica and the Guaymi Indians of Panama. In her words, "Young or old, rich or poor . . . God has placed each one of us on Planet Earth for such a time as this."

Stephanie has been married to her terrific and talented husband, Donald, for twenty-two years, and they have two wonderful sons plus a godly daughter-in-law. Stephanie and Donald live in Jacksonville, Florida.

About the Following God® Series

Three authors and fellow ministers, Wayne Barber, Eddie Rasnake, and Rick Shepherd, teamed up in 1998 to write a character-based Bible study for AMG Publishers. Their collaboration developed into the title, *Life Principles from the Old Testament.* Since 1998 these same authors and AMG Publishers have produced six more **character-based** studies—each consisting of twelve lessons geared around a five-day study of a particular Bible personality—the core of what is called the **Following God Character Series®**. In 2001, AMG Publishers launched a series of topical studies called the **Following God Discipleship Series®**. Soon after, books were released in the **Following God Christian Living Series™,** which is also topical in nature. The study you hold in your hand is part of the **Following God Through the Bible®** series, which is more of a verse-by-verse study. Though new studies and authors are being introduced, the interactive study format that readers have come to love remains constant with each new Following God® release. As new titles and categories are being planned, our focus remains the same: to provide excellent Bible study materials that point people to God's Word in ways that allow them to apply truths to their own lives. More information on this groundbreaking series can be found on the following web pages:

www.amgpublishers.com
www.followinggod.com

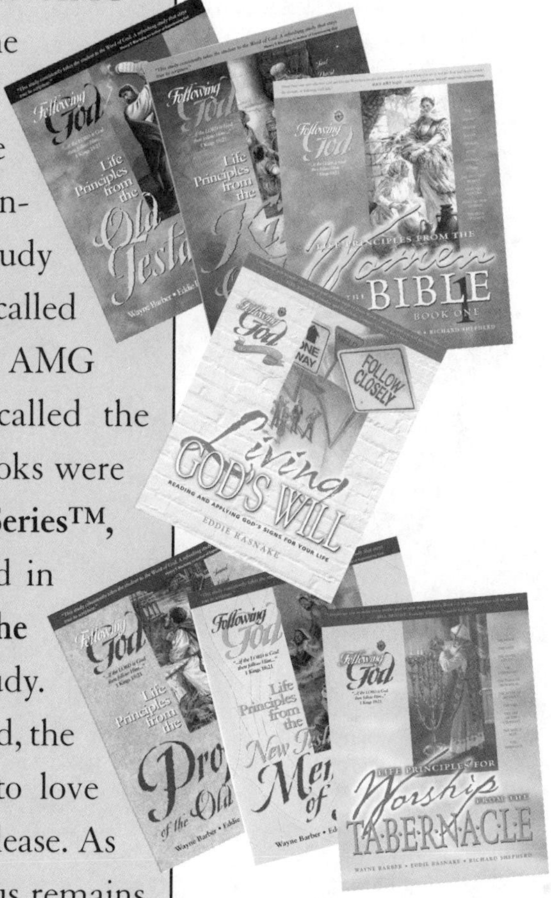

Preface

At the tender young age of twenty, most young men are just beginning to think about what they want to do with their lives, but Solomon's future was already mapped out for him. He was to become the king of Israel. When that time arrived, God spoke to him and said, "Ask! What shall I give you?"

Solomon didn't ask for wealth, nor did he ask to conquer his enemies . . . he didn't even ask for a long life. After evaluating himself in light of the responsibilities that lay before him, Solomon was wise enough to ask for wisdom.

As we study the book of Ecclesiastes we will also have the opportunity to study the author (Solomon), whom God inspired to pen this very interesting and often misunderstood book of the Bible. I pray we will gain much wisdom from the wisest man who ever lived. I often say that I like to learn from the mistakes of others rather than making my own. And I believe, although Solomon lived approximately three thousand years ago, that the lessons we can learn from him are just as relevant today as they were then. Times may have changed, but the heart of man has not.

The study of God's Word is necessary for our spiritual growth. It not only grounds us in our faith, but it also equips us for life's challenges and gives us adequate ammunition for each battle we face. Unfortunately, far too often we casually read God's Word. We skim the surface without realizing there is so much more.

After I came to know Jesus as my Savior, a minister at the church I attended gave me some very profound advice. He said, "There is a difference between the time you spend reading God's Word and the time you spend studying God's Word. . . . and you need to do both daily." My prayer is that, in studying God's Word, you will know Him more; in knowing Him more, you will love Him more; and in loving Him more, you will surrender to Him more.

This six-week study of Ecclesiastes is designed to give you a better understanding of this frequently avoided book. Each week, you will have five lessons and a memory verse. Each lesson will contain daily Scripture readings and various types of questions designed to examine the heart and inspire application. It has been said you only get out of things that which you are willing to put into them. That is also true with this Bible study. The Word of God has the power to change us, but we must be willing to spend time in it for that to occur. By reading the passages given and by answering the questions, you will have a better grasp of the biblical principles found in Ecclesiastes; you will also be challenged and encouraged to live out these principles in a practical way. So, for your own benefit, I strongly encourage your full participation for the next six weeks.

I will take most of the references from the New King James Version of the Bible (NKJV); many will be taken from the New American Standard Bible (NASB), while some will be taken from the Amplified and other versions. When using a version other than the New King James Bible, I will make a note of it beside the Scripture reference for your information.

As we embark upon this journey we will see the heart of every man written in the pages of Scripture. We will see our own heart and hopefully be challenged and encouraged to live a life of purpose and to understand what really matters most in this life we live, under the sun. Allow God to change you during this study of Ecclesiastes as Solomon makes his life an open book from which we can read and learn.

"Be diligent to present yourself approved to God, a worker who does not need to be ashamed, rightly dividing the word of truth." 2 Timothy 2:15 (NKJV)

"All Scripture is given by inspiration of God, and is profitable for doctrine, for reproof, for correction, for instruction in righteousness, that the man of God may be complete, thoroughly equipped for every good work." 2 Timothy 3:16, 17 (NKJV)

Stephanie Shott

Table of Contents

1

Life Lessons from History

A thorough study of Ecclesiastes involves a bit of a foundational history lesson. So we will spend this first week examining the early stages of Israel's government and her first three kings. It will be well worth our time, as we will glean many valuable life lessons along the way.

"Now all these things happened to them as examples, and they were written for our admonition . . ." (1 Corinthians 10:11)

"For whatever things were written before were written for our learning, . . ."
Romans 15:4

DAY 1	**Crying Out for a King (A Lesson in History)**
DAY 2	**Long Live the King (Saul)**
DAY 3	**The Model King (David)**
DAY 4	**Pointing Us to Jesus (David)**
DAY 5	**Considering a King (Solomon)**

MEMORY VERSE

"For I know the thoughts that I think toward you, says the LORD, thoughts of peace and not of evil, to give you a future and a hope."

Jeremiah 29:11

Life Lessons from History

DAY ONE

CRYING OUT FOR A KING

A Lesson in History

History really wasn't one of my favorite subjects in school. I just couldn't see the point of studying events that happened long before my time. Since I've become a Christian, however, I've become keenly aware of the importance of the lives and times of those who have gone before me. This week, allow yourself to benefit from the past as we get a foundational understanding of how Solomon became the king of what was called the United Monarchy of Israel and Judah.

Around 2,000 BC God called Abram to leave everything familiar and travel an uncharted course to an unknown destination. It was a call to trust and obey God. But that call came with a covenant, in which God promised Abram he would become the father of a great nation (Genesis 12:1, 2). Ultimately, that promise not only included the beginning of a nation, it consisted of God's plan to redeem mankind as well.

"I will make you a great nation . . ."
Genesis 12:2

The fulfillment of that promise began to unfold when Abraham and Sarah experienced the miraculous geriatric birth of Isaac. Isaac then married Rebekah, who gave birth to twin sons, Jacob and Esau. One night Jacob found himself in a divine wrestling match, where, in his desperate grip on the Living God, he found strength enough to plead for a blessing. God graciously answered his request by giving him a totally new identity. He would forevermore be known as Israel . . . the father of a nation. And so, a promise was fulfilled and a nation was born.

From the time God made His promise to Abram until the time Solomon became king, Israel underwent several transitions in power and governmental structure. Below is a timeline to help you see the transition from Abraham the Patriarch to Solomon the King.

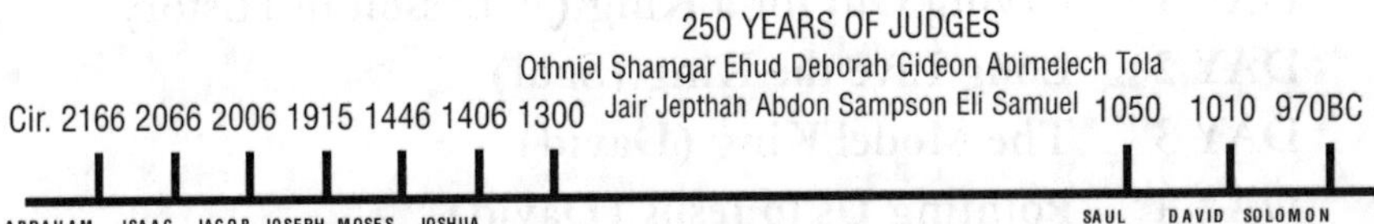

Initially, God assigned the Patriarchs—*Abraham, Isaac, and Jacob*—to lead His people. Joseph, one of Jacob's sons, soon took center stage as he brought this newfound nation, also known as *his family,* to Egypt to provide for them during a famine. After Joseph's death, the new king of Egypt feared the sheer numbers of Israelites and in an effort to protect his kingdom from potential overthrow, he placed the children of Israel in bondage. God then raised up Moses to deliver His people out of Egypt, and Joshua to lead them into the Promised Land.

As the nation grew and laws were defined, God began to use judges to lead His people. There was a period of approximately two hundred fifty years in which thirteen judges ruled the people through the leadership of the Lord in what is known as a *theocratic government.* Some of the judges were godly and wise; some of them were not.

Found last on the list of judges by divine decree was a prophet named Samuel. He was one of the good guys. If he had a middle name it would have been *Integrity.* His sons, Joel and Abijah, were next in line to embrace the title of judge, but, unfortunately, the apples fell very far from the tree. With the diabolical duo in charge, the elders of Israel began to fear what might happen. It was during that time they began to sneak a peek at the nations around them. Discontent with the possible outcome, they began to look for other options. That's when Israel began to cry out for a king.

🕮 Please read 1 Samuel 8:1–5. Why did the elders ask for a king instead of judges?

____

____

____

". . . and say, 'I will set a king over me like all the nations that are around me.'"

Deuteronomy 17:14

They wanted an opportunity to be like the other nations and have a king they could see, hear, and touch. We read this and we wonder, *What in the world were they thinking? God was their King!* But before we throw stones at the nation of Israel, it would be a good idea to reflect on our own lives. After all, isn't it human nature to want what others have?

As I sit here with my pen in hand and my own heart ready for a little self-examination, I'm reminded of several women I know who have paid a high price for "being discontent." Oh, sister, hear my heart! I may not have seen the cause, but I've often seen the effects and I truly want to convey how rocky the road can be when it begins with a discontent heart. I've learned from personal experience and from the experience of others there is no benefit to placing yourself in debt, just so you can keep up with your friends; the grass is *never* greener on the other side . . . in fact, it's just as weed-infested over there as it is where you are right now. I've seen too many women hurting, too many homes in a financial mess, and too many marriages suffering needlessly at the hands of a discontent heart. It may seem extreme, but if a discontent heart can cause Israel to cry out for a king at its own peril, what can it make you and me cry out for, and at what cost?

APPLY Circle the one that best describes your typical level of contentment:

VERY DISCONTENT SOMEWHAT DISCONTENT CONTENT VERY CONTENT

Is there a specific area in which you are finding it difficult to be content? If so, be willing to acknowledge it:

____

____

____

____

____

🕮 As we move forward in our history lesson, turn to 1 Samuel 8:6 and notice how Samuel handled Israel's irrational request. Summarize his response.

____

____

____

He certainly made it clear he was more than just a little miffed at their irrational request, but he also was careful not to let his anger spew out as senseless words. Samuel gave us a great example of how to deal with the foolishness of others as he took his frustration and their request straight to the Lord. I love how the New Living Translation phrases it: *"Samuel was displeased with their request and he went to the LORD for guidance."* We have a lot to learn from that one verse, don't we?! He didn't gossip or gripe; he didn't call a friend and tell him all the nitty-gritty details; he didn't rant and rave about how "wicked" they were. Samuel just prayed. Prayer brings wisdom and clarity; it brings peace and patience. Prayer often prevents us from running to others with someone else's business, cleverly disguising it as a prayer request.

APPLY Right now, is there anything you should be taking directly to God, rather than to others? Would you be willing to share it here?

Now, let's look at how God told Samuel to handle the situation. Please read 1 Samuel 8:7–18. What did the Lord tell Samuel to do?

What warning did God instruct Samuel to declare to the people?

We need to be very careful what we ask for . . . we might just get it.

The consequences of the people's desire to have a king "like all the other nations" far outweighed any benefit they would receive. God wanted them to know what they were in for if they continued to pursue their own king. In verses 10 through 18 we see that Samuel obeyed the Lord and gave them a very solemn warning. But according to verses 19 and 20, the people refused to listen and continued to cry out for a king.

Samuel had been a steadfast source of sound, godly guidance for many decades, but when they chose to close their ears to Samuel, they were, in effect, closing their ears to God. They were determined to have their own way and, unfortunately, they got exactly what they asked for. Have you ever known someone like that? Have you ever *been* someone like that?

We need to be very careful what we ask for . . . we might just get it. What a vital lesson for us to learn!

Sometimes we want our way more than we want to obey God. When our path seems more appealing to us than God's, it is evident we don't really understand His love. Our memory verse reminds us His love for us reaches into our very circumstances, so it's always in our best interest to choose His plan over our own. In Jeremiah 29:11, God tells us, *"For I know the thoughts that I think toward you, says the LORD, thoughts of peace and not of evil, to give you a future and a hope."* That truth is just as real for us today as it was for the nation of Israel.

Their refusal to listen to God's warning left them holding the "consequential bag." Consequences are part of the law of *cause and effect . . . sowing and reaping*. It's important to remember that it's not always a good thing to get what we ask for . . . especially when the Lord has warned us of the outcome. Choosing our own way instead of God's is never a good thing!

"Therefore he who rejects this does not reject man, but God, . . ."

I Thessalonians 4:8

APPLY As we finish today's lesson, I ask you to sincerely evaluate your life. Are there decisions you've made in the past irrespective of God's will? If so, what were they?

____

____

____

____

____

It can be very constructive to take a good, hard look at the way we've been living our lives and the decisions we've made. But once we've done that, we're forced to make another decision. Are we going to continue living the same self-directed and even misdirected way, or surrender to our heavenly Father? He has engraved us upon the palm of His hand. He eagerly awaits the homecoming of each and every prodigal. He stands—*no, He runs*—to welcome back all who have taken off in their own direction. If you've been running hard and fast in your own direction, I want to encourage you to hightail it back to your heavenly Father as fast as you can. He's waiting for you with His arms wide open!

Today, if you're struggling with a pivotal decision, I encourage you, my friend, to pry your fingers from your circumstances and let the Lord lead you according to His will. Allow the One who created you to have His perfect way in your life. He won't let you down!

Never allow yourself to have the misconception that you know better than God what is best for you.

Never allow yourself to have the misconception that you know better than God what is best for you.

As we conclude today's lesson, remember, our goal this week is to build a foundation on our way to Ecclesiastes. This will better help us understand Solomon's reign, his position, his responsibilities, his victories, his failures, and—most of all—his perspective, and what we learn along the way will be well worth our time.

Please write your memory verse for the week on a 3x5 card and don't forget to study it throughout the week!

"For I know the thoughts that I think toward you, says the LORD, thoughts of peace and not of evil, to give you a future and a hope." Jeremiah 29:11

MEMORY TIP
Take your weekly memory verse with you and review it at every stoplight. You'll be surprised how much you retain!

Life Lessons from History

DAY TWO

LONG LIVE THE KING!

Saul

For the next four days we are going to continue to step into the pages of biblical history as we get a glimpse of Israel's first three kings. As we look at three very different men, I believe we will see a little of ourselves in each of them. Today our attention will be on Saul, Israel's first choice for a king.

In 1 Samuel 10:1, Samuel reluctantly, but obediently, anointed Saul as king privately. Then, in 1 Samuel 10:24, Samuel anointed Saul publicly as the crowd cried out, "Long live the king!" Fast forward to 1 Samuel 12, where the scene is something like the swearing in of the president of the United States. It was Saul's coronation day and Samuel took his last opportunity to remind the people they had ultimately rejected the Lord. I wonder if Samuel was secretly hoping they would come to their senses.

📖 Please read 1 Samuel 8:7 and 12:12, 13. According to these verses, whom did the children of Israel reject when they asked for a king?

____

📖 Please read 1 Samuel 12:17. What did Samuel call their request for a king?

____

These passages puzzle my pea brain! Did they actually think they were making a good exchange? Did anyone in the group have the sense—or better yet, the heart—to cast their vote for the Lord? Why didn't Samuel's speech put the fear of God in them? The warning was clear, but it just didn't seem to matter. They were willing to suffer the consequences of rejecting the Lord all because they wanted something more tangible and so they could be like the other nations.

You may be surprised, but their sin was not necessarily that they desired to have a king. In fact, if you look with me at Deuteronomy 17:14, 15, you will see that God instructed the children of Israel how their government was to be established. He even told them the time would come when they would request a king, but He gave explicit instructions that it was to be a king of *His* choice, one from the tribe of Judah (Genesis 49:10). So, based on Scripture, their desire for a king was not the problem. The problem was really based on two core issues:

1) Their request for a king stemmed from a covetous heart. Look at 1 Samuel 8:19, 20: *"Nevertheless the people refused to obey the voice of Samuel; and they said, "No, but we will have a king over us, that we also may be like all the nations, and that our king may judge us and go out before us and fight our battles"* (NKJV). They obviously wanted to have what the other nations had—even to the point they were willing to allow a man to judge them and fight their battles in lieu of the Lord. Instead of keeping up with the Joneses, they wanted to keep up with the nations. So they cried out for a king—and that's exactly what they got.

2) They wanted to choose who would reign over them rather than accepting God's choice for them. Remember what 1 Samuel 12:13 says? *"Now therefore, here is the king whom you have chosen* and *whom you have desired."* They obviously wanted to make their own decisions, so they made the foolish mistake of alienating themselves from the God who had always been on their side ... the One who had been their shelter and their defense ... the One who had fought their battles for them and had brought them one victory after another. There's no record of anyone asking God for wisdom. There's no mention of prayer and fasting for the Lord's direction. Like ordering a burger from a drive-thru, they wanted it now and they wanted it their way.

Their request for a king stemmed from a covetous heart.

Sometimes, we desire what is tangible because it *seems* more real to us. Yet the tangible seldom requires very much faith. For centuries, the faith of the children of Israel had been validated by the abiding presence, protection, and direction of the Lord. You would think they would have sensed a great deal of security and peace knowing Jehovah God was their King. Unfortunately, like many of us, their memories were short and their faith was small, so they knowingly and willingly began to chart a course for dangerous waters.

Let's shift gears and turn our attention to Saul. His name, very fittingly, means "Asked." Saul was the king Israel "Asked" for! (I can't help but laugh about this!) In 1 Samuel 9:2, Saul is described as the most handsome man in all Israel. I'm sure he made the cover of the Israelite Times as "Mr. Benjamite." He may have made the cover, but his story lacks character ... and so did he.

📖 Please read the following verses and you will see why Israel may have thought Saul would be a good king.

1 Samuel 9:5 – Whom was Saul concerned about?

____

____

1 Samuel 9:21 – What type of attitude does Saul demonstrate?

____

____

1 Samuel 11:12–15 – In verse 12, some wanted those who opposed Saul to be put to death. How did Saul respond in verse 13?

____

____

First impressions aren't always reliable, are they? In 1 Samuel 11:13–15 Saul appeared to be a man who would lead Israel to follow God and give Him the glory for the battles they would win. He demonstrated his courage when he prevailed in the battle against the Ammonites. He seemed to start out on the right foot, but as we look a little further into Saul's life we'll see he wasn't such a good choice after all.

📖 Please read 1 Samuel 10:6, 9–11. What was Saul given and what did he do?

____

____

____

____

God had given Saul another heart. In the Hebrew the term "another heart" signifies he had been given a heart *completely different* from the one he had before. He had also been given the Holy Spirit. In the Old Testament, the Holy Spirit would empower certain people to accomplish God's specific purpose with God's power and wisdom. This, of course, did not mean those who had the Spirit of God on their lives would always choose to honor the Lord. However, it did mean they had the capacity to do so. Saul had been given another heart and the ability, through the Holy Spirit, to accomplish all the things God purposed for him.

📖 Please read 1 Samuel 10:8. What did Samuel tell Saul to do?

____

____

____

In 1 Samuel 13:8–12, what did Saul do and what was his reason for doing it?

Disobedience always comes with a price tag.

____

____

____

____

In 1 Samuel 13:13, 14, what were the consequences of Saul's impulsive act?

____

____

____

Disobedience always comes with a price tag. Saul's arrogance kicked in and he chose to do things his way instead of listening to the man of God, Samuel. There's a popular song titled, "I Did It My Way." Well, that may sound good in the lyrics of a song, but it's not the best way to live our lives. "Our way" isn't always the best way. We're human and prone to making mistakes. We are drawn away from God by our flesh and, unfortunately, we tend to want what isn't good for us. So, when all is said and done, I would much rather have the lyrics of my song say, *"I Did It* His *Way."* Wouldn't you?

Again, we're looking at consequences. But this time, we're looking at Saul's. Remember, sin always costs us something. You've probably heard the saying, "Sin takes us farther than we want to go, makes us stay longer than we want to stay, and makes us pay far more than we're willing to pay." Saul's fall is a reminder of the consequences of disobedience and the destruction of sin. He was a man who had it all and lost it because of a disobedient and arrogant heart. He was the first king of Israel and could have set the standard for leadership. Instead, he was an inept, inadequate, and contemptible king. In 1 Samuel 16:14 we read that his worst nightmare became his reality when the Spirit of the Lord left him. Saul remained king for many years after that, but his attempts at governing were futile. He was a miserable man and a dishonorable king.

Before we conclude our lesson, I'd like for you to see a few snapshots of Saul's life so you'll better understand why Saul turned out to be such a bad king.

Event	Scripture Reference
On more than one occasion, Saul ordered the death of his own son Jonathan.	1 Samuel 14:44; 20:33
In disobedience to God's command, Saul spared wicked King Agag (king of the Amalekites) and chose the "best" of the spoils from the war.	1 Samuel 15:9
Saul made David his target, repeatedly trying to kill him.	1 Samuel 18:11, 21–25; 19:1,10,15; 20:31)
Saul's jealousy of David spawned a killing spree, where he murdered the priests of the temple and a host of innocent people in Nob.	1 Samuel 22:16–19
Saul sought the counsel of a sorcerer at En Dor.	1 Samuel 28:7, 8

It has been said good men begin well, but great men finish well. Many times we see our brothers and sisters in Christ fly out of the starting blocks of Christianity at record pace only to fizzle out or fall. It is the desire of my heart (and I'm sure it is your desire also) to finish faithfully. That requires determination. It is a constant choice of the will. Each wise choice brings us one step closer to faithfully finishing the course. Saul's life is a living, breathing example of what can happen when we choose our own way.

"Fight the good fight of faith, lay hold on eternal life, . . ."

I Timothy 6:12

Saul hasn't been the most honorable man to study, but don't you just love how comprehensive the Word of God is? It shows us the good, the bad, and the ugly! Romans 15:4 tells us, *"For whatever things were written before were written for our learning. . . "* (NKJV). May we learn from Israel to guard ourselves against a discontent heart; may we learn from Samuel to take everything to the Lord in prayer; and may we learn from Saul it is not so much how well we start, but how well we finish that really matters.

Ask the Lord to help you stay focused on Him, His Word, and His will so you can faithfully finish the course He has for you.

MEMORY VERSE

"For I know the thoughts that I think toward you, says the LORD, thoughts of peace and not of evil, to give you a future and a hope."

Jeremiah 29:11

MEMORY TIP

Tape your memory verse card to your bathroom mirror and review it while you're getting ready!

Life Lessons from History

DAY THREE

". . . The LORD has sought for himself a man after His own heart, . . ."

I Samuel 13:14

THE MODEL KING

David

Throughout Scripture, God has said of only one man, *"He is a man after my own heart"* . . . and that was David. He is also the only man in Scripture to be given the name David, which very appropriately means "beloved." For the next two days we will have the opportunity to study the life of David . . . God's choice for Israel's king.

📖 Let's begin by reading Psalm 63:1:
(A verse written by David while he was in the wilderness of Judea)

"O God, You are *my God; Early will I seek You;*
My soul thirsts for You; My flesh longs for You
In a dry and thirsty land where there is no water."

As we start today's lesson please take a moment and pray that the Lord will give you a heart like David's . . . one that longs for the Living God.

If I were to describe David's life, I might give you a rags-to-riches story . . . or maybe a story about an underdog. I might depict him as some sort of superhero, or maybe he'd be found in the pages of a romance or suspense novel. He was certainly quite the complex character. But rather than primarily focusing on David's life today, I think it would do us good to get a glimpse of his heart.

Through the years, many theologians have shared various viewpoints as to why God said David was a man after His own heart. Some say it was David's courageous faith as he pegged Goliath with a pebble, sending the Philistines fleeing. Some believe it was his willingness and readiness to repent, especially in light of his foolish fling with Bathsheba and his murderous cover-up. Some say it was his trust in the Lord and his love for mercy and righteousness as he spared Saul and left his promised role as king in the Lord's hands. Others think it was his desire to please the Lord by building Him a temple, and his heart of praise in the songs he wrote. Most agree it is all of the above and so much more.

Join me as we travel through the Psalms and find David pouring his heart out to God. Maybe in the process, we will be one step closer to having a heart like his. Pay close attention to the lessons for *your* heart you may learn from David's. We'll begin with:

David's Heart of Repentance

📖 Please read Psalm 51:1–13, then rewrite the first phrase of the first verse.

____

____

____

David's cry for mercy is set against the backdrop of his sin with Bathsheba and his murder of her husband. With Nathan's finger pointing at him, the weight of his sin became too much to bear. His guilt was only equaled by his shame. Yes, he was the man! David understood that the only place he could run for mercy was to the One he had ultimately sinned against. Like the tax collector in Luke 18:13, he cried out to the Living God for mercy.

How about you? Do you readily repent the moment the Spirit of God points out your sin to you? Do you quickly run to the Lord for mercy?

In verse 10, David asks, *"Create in me a clean heart, O God, and renew a steadfast spirit within me."* The word *clean* means "pure, capable of being used in, or taking part in religious rituals of Israel." The word *steadfast* means "ready or prepared for use, fixed." When we sin against God, our guilt and shame render us useless and, in our own eyes, unfit to serve the Lord. Our sense of unworthiness is like taking the batteries out of the remote control. It's useless, and so are we when we're carrying around our guilt and shame as if we have a 50-pound sack of potatoes on our shoulders.

David cried out to God to have mercy on him, to create in him a pure heart, prepared for service to the Most High God. He understood he needed cleansing from his sin, he needed forgiveness and restoration. He had lost the joy of his salvation. So he humbled himself before a holy and righteous God as he cried out in sincere repentance and, in so doing, he left us a beautiful picture of what it means to have a heart of repentance.

Now let's look at David's trust in and his praise to the Lord.

📖 Please read Psalm 3:3–6. Are you confident the Lord hears you and sustains you as He did David? __________

Do you remember a time the Lord lifted up your head? If so, please share that here.

____

____

____

____

____

____

📖 Please read Psalm 8:3, 4. David understood the greatness of God in contrast with the smallness of us. It caused him to stand in awe to realize God would even think about us. Would you take a moment and stand in awe of our Savior and our God? You may want to write your thoughts.

"I cried to the LORD with my voice, And He heard me from His holy hill,"

Psalm 3:4

📖 Finally, read Psalm 103:1–5. David's song of praise unto the Lord echoes through the portals of time into our current songbooks. His love for and trust in the Lord just overflowed into songs of praise. As I read these verses, I can almost hear his heart.

Dear sister, have you ever blessed the Lord with all you've got?

Have you ever gone through a list of things He's done for you, as David did?

Now is your chance. In the back of this book, write a prayer or song of praise to the Lord. Then say it (or sing it) out loud and bless the Lord with all that is within you! This may just be the day you get a little bit closer to having a heart like David's!

The 411

Now let's get the 411 (information) on David. He was the second and most important king of Israel. His reign is known as the "Golden Age" and today, he is still known as the "Model King." He began his adolescence as a shepherd boy, but his life was divinely interrupted when God called him to become the second king of Israel. He was from the tribe of Judah and the youngest of Jesse's eight sons. His great-grandparents were Ruth and Boaz (Ruth 4:17–22). The genealogy of David is an important aspect of his significance. While the Old Testament gives a concise family tree of David in 1 Chronicles 2:3–15, the New Testament gives the lineage of David in Matthew 1:1–6 and Luke 3:31–38. Both references in the New Testament are part of the genealogy of Jesus Christ. Tomorrow we'll have the opportunity to study the significance of David, his genealogy, and his relationship to Christ.

The chart below may help you see a summary of David's life. Much like a view from a plane, we can see a general overview, but we really can't see the details.

Fact/Event	Scripture Reference
David was from Bethlehem.	1 Samuel 16:1
He was a handsome shepherd boy.	1 Samuel 16:11, 12
He was privately anointed king by Samuel.	1 Samuel 16:13
He was a musician.	1 Samuel 16:17, 18, 23

Fact/Event	Scripture Reference
He was strong and brave and killed Goliath.	1 Samuel 17:34-37, 44-53
David fled from Saul's relentless attempts to kill him.	1 Samuel 18:11; 19:18; 23:15, 24–26
He married Saul's daughter Michal.	1 Samuel 16:13
He was befriended by Saul's son Jonathan.	1 Samuel 16:17, 18, 23
He spared Saul's life more than once.	1 Samuel 24:2–12; 26:5–12
He married Abigail and Ahinoam.	1 Samuel 25:42, 43
He was formally anointed king of Judah.	2 Samuel 2:4, 11
He was formally anointed king of Israel.	2 Samuel 5:1–5
He brought the Ark of the Covenant to Jerusalem.	2 Samuel 6:2, 12–19
He committed adultery and murder.	2 Samuel 11:2–5, 14, 15
He was confronted with his sin and repented.	2 Samuel 12:7–13
He spoke his last words to his son Solomon.	1 Kings 2:1–11

Although we missed a lot of details by condensing David's life down to a list of important events, at least our aerial view enabled us to get a snapshot of a man after God's own heart. Amid the insecurities of his youth and his indiscretions as a man, he continued to passionately serve the Living God!

"'I have found David the son of Jesse, a man after My own heart, who will do all My will.'"

Acts 13:22

As David progressed in years and it was time to think about passing the kingly baton, he began to convey to Solomon the need to finish a project near and dear to his father's heart. It was the building of the temple. You see, David deeply desired to build the temple for the Lord but, because his life was marked by war and bloodshed, God would not allow him to do so (2 Samuel 7:5,13; 1 Chronicles 28:3). However, as we see David's fervent desire to do something great for God accompanied by the understanding he wouldn't be able to complete it, we find a wonderful example of how to gracefully pass our own batons.

In 1 Chronicles 29:1–9 we find David giving Solomon instructions and calling on the children of Israel to give to the "Temple Building Fund." Sometimes, in our zeal to accomplish something for God, we get so caught up in seeing it through to the end that we begin to take ownership of the "ministry" and we're too busy to hear the voice of God as He gently whispers, "This is for someone else now." There is a bittersweet joy in passing the baton. David has left us a beautiful legacy of understanding the concept of preparing others to continue the ministries the Lord has initiated through us, and then accepting the responsibility to turn our ministries over to those whom God has chosen to complete them.

David truly was a man after God's own heart. He is responsible for writing at least seventy-five of the one hundred fifty Psalms, and the Bible calls him "the sweet psalmist of Israel (2 Samuel 23:1 KJV). David's name is mentioned more than one thousand times throughout the Bible. He is an extremely important biblical and historical figure, yet his humanness gives us hope that no matter how far we may fall, God can still use us.

David was just an ordinary guy whom God used in an extraordinary way. He was usually brave, yet sometimes afraid (like many of us); he was for the most part strong, yet weak in some areas (like many of us). He was talented and sensitive, yet he was truly a warrior. He was real, he was fallible and flawed—just like you and me—but God still chose to make him king. As we keep his humanity in mind, let's take a look at David's journey from shepherd boy to king and see what lessons we can learn in the process.

He was real, he was fallible and flawed—just like you and me—

📖 Please read 2 Samuel 7:8 and Psalms 78:71, 72.
What did God call David from?

____

____

____

What did God call David to?

____

____

____

What prior training did David have?

____

____

____

Just a quick glance at your local classifieds will quickly reveal the emphasis our culture places on education. Even a file clerk needs an associate's degree these days. We're trained to believe we have to have some type of formal training to prepare us for all the things God desires us to do. Now, I'm not underestimating the importance of training and education, but sometimes, God just calls us from tending sheep and puts us to work tending souls.

David had on-the-job training in his transition from shepherding sheep to shepherding God's people, but it didn't happen overnight. Samuel privately anointed him king when he was about fifteen years old, but it wasn't until he was thirty he actually became Judah's king. He then had to wait another seven-and-a-half years before he took his rightful role as king of all Israel.

Tucked not so neatly in the pages of Israel's history is the reign of Saul's son, Ish-bosheth. His turbulent two-year reign tragically ended when he was murdered by two of his own captains. There is much speculation as to what happened during the five-and-a-half-year period between the time Ish-bosheth was killed and David took his rightful role as king. But this we know: God's promise was finally fulfilled and David became king of the United Monarchy of Israel and Judah.

God did not waste one minute of David's twenty-two-and-a-half-year wait. These were formative years for the Model King. Our heavenly Father often uses the circumstances of our lives to prepare us for the roles He calls us to that are beyond us. In David we see a shepherd boy become a warrior; we watch an attendant in Saul's court spend a decade fleeing for his life; we catch a glimpse of Judah's king taking the lead in a civil war that lasted seven-and-a-half years. Waiting twenty-two-and-a-half years to see a promise fulfilled would be extremely challenging. I wonder if David ever thought his failures had changed God's plan.

You may feel as if you are in God's waiting room or that what you are doing now is monotonous and unproductive. I encourage you, my friend, do whatever you are doing *now* for the glory of God. This may just be your training ground!

David's humble existence as a shepherd boy was radically changed the moment God chose him as king. But I want you to see this beautiful parallel: The Bible tells us in Revelation 1:6, *"[He] has made us kings and priests. . . ."* WOW! He takes our meager existence and exalts us to royalty—just as he did with David. And that's not all, my sister! You see, just as He called David to shepherd His people, He calls us to do the same in the sphere of influence He has given us. Whether you realize it or not, God called you to shepherd someone. It may be your children or Sunday school class or maybe some of your friends and co-workers, but the fact is, you are shepherding someone.

So, from the depths of my heart, I pray you will see the importance of guarding your flock diligently. In Acts 20:28 (NASB), God told the elders of the Ephesian church, *"Be on guard for yourselves and for all the flock, among which the Holy Spirit has made you overseers, to shepherd the church of God which He purchased with His own blood."* I believe that that verse applies to us as well, for God has made each of us shepherds of little flocks all around us.

Today we have had the opportunity to glance at David's life, his strengths and weaknesses, and his twenty-two-and-a-half-year course on "Kingship 101." We've also seen our own responsibility to carefully shepherd those God has entrusted to us.

Dear friend, God knows our strengths and our weaknesses, He knows what we are going through, and He desires that we persevere in the lessons of life so we may truly live to our fullest potential for His glory.
I encourage you . . . be moldable clay in His loving hands!

I encourage you . . . be moldable clay in His loving hands!

P.S. Have you worked on your memory verse today? Here it is again!

"For I know the thoughts that I think toward you, says the LORD, thoughts of peace and not of evil, to give you a future and a hope."
Jeremiah 29:11

MEMORY TIP
Choose a family member or friend who may need encouragement and ask them if you can practice saying your memory verse out loud to them. You'll be amazed at the power of God's Word to encourage them!

Life Lessons from History

DAY FOUR

POINTING US TO JESUS

David

Reading through God's Word, I am constantly amazed at the many ways God has chosen to make His plan so very clear to us. One of those ways is called *typology.* Typology comes from the Greek word *typos*, which means "a blow or a mark left by a blow; a pattern or imprint." Typology uses a literal person, place, or thing to represent a spiritual person, place, or thing. It prefigures or foreshadows something else. Because Jesus is the central interwoven theme throughout the Word of God, much of the typology threaded throughout the Bible is a direct reference to Jesus Christ. For instance, in the Old Testament, the sacrificial law was implemented by God. It was a Jewish mandate to shed the blood of a lamb for the covering of sin. It actually was a foreshadow, a typology, of the shedding of the blood of the Lamb of God, Jesus Christ, in order to cleanse us from our sin.

Today, we'll look at one of the most vital roles David plays in Scripture, and that is how he is a "type" (a prefigurement, a foreshadower) of Christ.

It all started in Genesis 49 when Jacob called his boys in for the blessing of their lives. In verse 10 he said, *"The scepter shall not depart from Judah, Nor the ruler's staff from between his feet, Until Shiloh comes; And to him* shall be *the obedience of the peoples."* (NASB) The name *Shiloh* indicates "He whose it is, Messiah, the Peaceful One." From the first book of the Bible, the promise was made Messiah would come from the tribe of Judah. Shiloh was to be the One sent to accomplish the will of God, which, fortunately for us, is the salvation of mankind.

Let's establish our foundation for today's lesson by exploring David's lineage found in Matthew 1:1–17. Now I know we frequently tend to skim over the genealogies as insignificant information, but today, I think you'll discover their importance and enjoy learning the connection King David has with King Jesus. When you're done reading through David's family tree, look at the following verses and see if you can identify how David is a "type" of Christ. Pay close attention to the parallel application of these verses.

David: Psalm 31:11–13 ______________________________

Jesus: Isaiah 53:3 ______________________________

David: Psalm 78:70–72 ______________________________

Jesus: John 10:11,14; Hebrews 13:20 ______________________________

David: Psalm 89:27 ______________________________

Jesus: Colossians 1:15; Revelation 17:14 ______________________________

David: 1 Chronicles 17:12 ______________________________

Jesus: Hebrews 1:8 ______________________________

"But to the Son He says, 'Your throne, O God, is forever and ever; . . .'"

Hebrews 1:8

Now we're going to dig a little deeper! In many of the verses given below, David's name is used, but Jesus is the One to whom the verse actually refers. As you read them, keep in mind that Hosea lived 300 years after David, and Ezekiel lived 493 years after David. So remember, David had died long before these prophecies were ever made. As you read each verse please explain who you think it refers to and why.

Jeremiah 30:9

____

____

Ezekiel 34:23, 24

____

____

Ezekiel 37:24

____

____

Hosea 3:5

____

____

God's Word contains numerous verses that use David to point us to Jesus through prophecy and typology. However, I'd like to share with you one specific use of typology in which David foreshadows the Lord Jesus Christ, and that is through his name.

The name David means "*the beloved one*." Its definition is further expressed as "*the one in whom I have delight*." What a beautiful typology of our Lord Jesus Christ! As I was reading this out loud, it resounded with familiarity. Take a quick trip with me to Matthew 3:16, 17 (NASB) and I think you'll see why.

Talk about holy water! Never before has water been made more holy than it was that day when the Creator of the Universe set his completely divine / completely human foot on the banks of the Jordan River. John's reluctant baptism of the Son of God concluded when the heavenly Father broke the silence of the moment and uttered these amazing and authenticating words: "*This is My beloved Son, in whom I am well-pleased.*" This wonderful parallel just overflows with the powerful love of God! Do you see how Jesus is woven throughout the Bible? Do you see how God has carefully given us a picture of Jesus throughout the Word of God? We serve an awesome God, don't we?! He has made Himself known to us in ways we have yet to discover.

". . . This is My beloved Son, in whom I am well-pleased."

Matthew 3:17

God had promised His people a king who would reign forever. The Jewish people knew He would be a descendant of David. He would be the Shepherd King: *The Beloved Son of God in whom He is well-pleased*. Jesus was the fulfillment of that promise. Acts 13:22, 23 says,

> *"And when He had removed him, He raised up for them David as king, to whom also He gave testimony and said, 'I have found David the son of Jesse,*

a man after My own heart, who will do all My will.' From this man's seed, according to the promise, God raised up for Israel a Savior—Jesus."

Are you surprised by the way God used a shepherd boy to so profoundly point others to Jesus? It is the heart of God we not only all be pointed to Jesus, but that we, who know Him personally, point others to Jesus as well. It is the deepest desire of my heart to do exactly that . . . point others to Jesus . . . by my words and by the actions and reactions of my life. I pray that is your deepest desire also.

P.S. Don't forget to work on your memory verse today!
"For I know the thoughts that I think toward you, says the LORD, thoughts of peace and not of evil, to give you a future and a hope." Jeremiah 29:11 (NKJV)

MEMORY TIP
Take the time to say the verse three times out loud!

Life Lessons from History

DAY FIVE

CONSIDERING A KING

Solomon

Through the years books have been written and movies have been made to dramatize the adventures of King Solomon, the unparalleled wealth that induced adulation, and the idolatrous women who led him astray. Today, we finally have the opportunity to pull back the curtains on the stage of Solomon's life. We'll begin with his birth, move on to his famous request for wisdom, and conclude with some mistakes he made along the way.

As we buckle up for a ride through Solomon's life, it's good to know that Solomon started out on the right foot. Unfortunately, he didn't cross the finish line nearly as well as he left the starting blocks. My prayer is that this study will help us get a better understanding of what matters most so we will finish well.

The 411 on Solomon
Solomon was the secondborn son of David and Bathsheba. He was the third king of the United Monarchy of Israel and Judah, and the wisest man to ever live (other than Jesus, of course).

📖 As we examine three specific events that influenced Solomon's life, please look up each Scripture passage and answer the questions.

Solomon's Birth: 2 Samuel 12:24, 25
David named his new son *Solomon* ("Peaceable"), however, Nathan called him *Jedidiah*, which means "Beloved of the Lord." Why do you think Nathan called Solomon *Jedidiah*? (There are no wrong answers.)

____

____

____

Gracefully inscribed in these two wonderful verses are two very telling names. The name *Solomon* gives us a prophetic glance at the peace Solomon would experience throughout most of his reign as king. The name *Jedidiah* presents the ever present agape love God demonstrated to David. Solomon reminds us that God desires to accomplish His perfect plan in and through us regardless of our background–in spite of where we've been and what our past may whisper in our ears. Jedidiah conveys a steadfast love that shines through the darkness of our sin and loves us because of whose we are, not because of what we have done. Just as God chose His *beloved* David to rule the nation of Israel, He would also use His *beloved* Jedidiah to do the same.

Verse 24 ends with the statement, *"Now the LORD loved him."* Oh, how vast is the goodness and mercy of God! Many may have written David and Bathsheba off. How could anything good come from something so steeped in sin? Adultery and murder are definitely *not* building blocks to a good and blessed marriage.

Romans 8:28 (NASB) tells us, *"And we know that God causes all things to work together for good to those who love God, to those who are called according to His purpose."* This verse doesn't mean God causes us to sin in order to bring about some "good" thing in the end. It does mean, however, that God's love *for* us and His goodness *to* us transcend our ability to mess things up.

Trials and tribulations are a real part of our existence. Because we're all human and life happens, it is inevitable we will go through difficulties (John 16:33). But there are other times when we are engulfed in the consequences of our own fleshly choices and are overwhelmed by the trials we have placed ourselves in. It is important for us to know that even in our self-inflicted circumstances, God still loves us and will work out all things for our good.

In Romans 8:28, the phrase "work together" gives us a picture of a Master Weaver as He weaves together a beautiful tapestry. Each strand, in and of itself, may not be so beautiful, but the final result is breathtaking. We have strands of our lives that are visibly ugly and unpleasant, but as God weaves our lives together, He makes them beautiful and useful. Ecclesiastes 3:11 tells us He makes everything beautiful in its time. That is what He did for David and Bathsheba when He gave them Solomon. That is what He did for you and me when He saved us, and that is what He continues to do for us as His children.

Solomon's Request: 1 Kings 3:5–14
In verse 7, what two things did Solomon call himself?

____

____

📖 Please read Mark 10:13–16. What did Jesus say one had to be like in order to receive the kingdom of God?

____

____

____

____

"And we know that God causes all things to work together for good to those who love God, to those who are called according to His purpose."

Romans 8:28 (NASB)

". . . You have made Your servant king instead of my father David, but I am a little child . . ."

I Kings 3:7

Solomon was humble enough to have a child-size view of himself and was childlike enough to believe God would grant him the wisdom he needed to effectively rule the nation. James 1:5–7 explains that the acquisition of wisdom must be preceded by the activation of faith—faith that believes that God is who He says He is and will do what He says He'll do—childlike faith.

Solomon quickly acknowledged his immaturity and inexperience. Humility and faith were the foundations of his request for wisdom. He was wise enough to ask for wisdom, humble enough to recognize his own inability and He trusted God enough to call upon Him for help. Perhaps that's why God chose to make him the wisest man in history.

When I was a little girl, I went to a public pool and courageously jumped into the deep end. It wasn't really courageous—it was stupid. I had learned to swim about three years prior, but hadn't swum a stroke since. I knew I was taking a big chance when I took the plunge, but I didn't want to admit I really couldn't swim. Good thing there was a boy who realized I was going under and reached out and rescued me. (Otherwise, you wouldn't be reading this.)

Sometimes, we won't go to God and ask for wisdom because we're too busy treading our circumstantial waters to think right. Perhaps we don't want to confess our inabilities . . . we want to appear as though we can handle it. Maybe others might not think we're as spiritual or qualified as we want them to think. But crying out to God for wisdom is sure a lot better than drowning in your own pride.

When we're willing to humble ourselves under the mighty hand of God, He will exalt us in due time and give us the wisdom we so desperately need. He promises! Let Solomon be an example of how to gain the wisdom of God by acknowledging our own lack of wisdom and then by humbly asking God for His.

"Therefore humble yourselves under the mighty hand of God, that He may exalt you in due time."

I Peter 5:6

In 1 Kings 3:8 Solomon confesses he is in the midst of people, whom _______________ had chosen.

Solomon requests wisdom. Why does he make this request?

____

____

In verse 10, Solomon's speech _____________ the Lord. (Remember what Hebrews 11:6 says?)

In verses 11–14 we see that God blessed Solomon with wisdom, but He also blessed Solomon with three other things. What were the other blessings promised to Solomon? ___________________, ___________________, ____________________

Which was conditional?

____

Did you notice that God unconditionally blessed Solomon with riches and honor, yet, his hope for a long life would be in direct correlation to his obedience to God's Law? The promises of God are wrapped in two very distinct packages: conditional and unconditional. Scripture is chock-full of unconditional promises for His children. Those promises are ours because we have become joint heirs with Jesus Christ through the new birth. The other package of promises isn't quite as easy to unwrap, because they are conditional. That is, they are ours if we have become His children through the new birth (John 3:3), *but* in order to claim those promises, we must meet the conditions God places upon us.

Dear friend, in order to know which promises are conditional and which ones are unconditional, we must spend time in God's Word. The more time we spend with Him—in prayer and in His Word—the more we will know Him and the more we will know the blessings He has for us. If you'd like to expand your promise arsenal, use highlighters of two different colors whenever you read the Word. Use one color for the conditional promises and the other color for the unconditional ones. Then, every time you look at a page in your Bible, you'll have the precious reminders of God's promises staring you in the face and you'll know immediately if they are conditional or unconditional.

If you've been struggling with spending quality time in the Word, I would like to encourage you to be like Nike and "just do it." It's really not about *having* enough time, it's about *making* enough time. If we don't, our faith will vacillate like the waves of the ocean. We'll be up one minute and down the next. Our faith will be weak and our testimonies will be in jeopardy. So, I encourage you, dear one, *just do it.* Set aside time to read and study His Word. You'll be the one to benefit from it.

Now, let's move on and see where Solomon went wrong.

Solomon's Poor Choices

Solomon's life is proof that wisdom doesn't necessarily equal perfection. He may have been the wisest man to ever live, but he blew it big time! You see, God had given specific requirements for those who were to be king of Israel. Two requirements are listed in Deuteronomy 17:17 (NASB): *"He shall not multiply wives for himself, or else his heart will turn away; nor shall he greatly increase silver and gold for himself."* In Deuteronomy 7:3, 4, God forbids the children of Israel to marry outside their own nationality to prevent idol worship from infiltrating the camp.

Solomon's life is proof that wisdom doesn't necessarily equal perfection.

Unfortunately, Solomon was much like his daddy, David, and what David did in moderation, Solomon did to excess. How else could you possibly explain seven hundred wives and three hundred concubines (1 Kings 11:3)? That poor man couldn't have known what he was getting himself into. Perhaps he wasn't wise enough to know that a thousand women in one household was definitely not a good idea. I wonder how he survived the sea of hormones or if he ever got a word in edgewise?

First Kings 11:4 (NASB) tells us, *"For it came about when Solomon was old, his wives turned his heart away after other gods; and his heart was not wholly devoted to the LORD his God, as the heart of David his father had been* And that's exactly what happened. The wisest human being who ever lived foolishly turned away from God and began a life of idolatry . . . just as the Lord had warned.

God knows what's best. He doesn't give us commandments just to see if we will obey; they're for our good. We must continually choose whether we will obey God, or be like Solomon and walk in wisdom for much of our lives and then be disloyal to our precious Lord. Remember—many begin strong, few truly finish faithfully. Ask God to help you be one of the faithful few.

Let's take a moment and review some of the valuable and practical lessons we learned today from Solomon's life:

God is the Master Weaver. We can rest in the fact He will create a beautiful masterpiece from each strand of our life.

True wisdom comes from God, and when we seek Him, it should always be with an attitude of humility and faith.

God gives us commands for our own good. It is for our eternal (as well as temporal) benefit to obey Him rather than choose to live according to the dictates of our flesh.

Which of these lessons speaks to your heart and your circumstances today, and how can you apply it to your life?

P.S. Do you have this week's verse memorized? I hope so! What a wonderful promise to each of us!

"For I know the thoughts that I think toward you, says the LORD, thoughts of peace and not of evil, to give you a future and a hope." Jeremiah 29:11 (NKJV)

2

From Vanity to Victory

Today, we find ourselves at the threshold of Ecclesiastes and as we begin our journey into the pages of wisdom, we will have the privilege of sitting at the feet of the wisest man to ever live: Solomon. This week we will get a glimpse of Solomon's perspective as we look at his quest for a meaningful life under the sun.

We will be challenged to look at our own lives under the microscope of God's Word and we will find hope for the hurting heart.

"Vanity of vanities," says the Preacher, "Vanity of vanities! All is vanity."

Ecclesiastes 1:2

MEMORY VERSE

"Therefore if you have been raised up with Christ, keep seeking the things above, where Christ is, seated at the right hand of God. Set your mind on things above, not on things that are on earth"
Colossians 3:1, 2 (NASB)

From Vanity to Victory

DAY ONE

WHAT'S IT ALL MEAN?

Ecclesiastes 1:1–7

I remember when the Lord impressed upon my heart the strong desire to write this book. God had called Donald and me to the mission field, and we were in the process of watching all our material possessions leave our carport as garage sale items for what ended up to be pocket change. That really didn't bother me because I've never been a "stuff" kind of girl. The struggle came when I looked my 18-year-old son in the eyes and told him we were moving to Costa Rica. He didn't feel led to go, but how could we leave him? He was so young! What if he got sick? What if his car broke down? Who would help him? What about my mom? What about Donald's mom? I just wanted to make sense of it all. I knew God's call was real, but I also knew the hurt in their heart, and mine was just as real.

Although I trusted that God would use our absence to grow our son in ways not possible if we were to stay, I just really needed some clarity . . . I needed the Lord to shed some eternal light on my circumstances. It was during those turbulent days, when my maternal heart was wrestling with the details of God's call, the Lord led me to Ecclesiastes. I was intrigued by Solomon's search for significance and his own need for clarity. At the end of his quest he had a very clear picture of what really mattered most in this life we all live, under the sun. I knew I needed that same kind of perspective. Not only for that moment in time, but for each day and each decision. I knew I really wanted an unshakable understanding of what matters most.

Did You Know?
HEBREW POETRY

Ecclesiastes is one of the poetical books of the Old Testament, Hebrew poetry is unique in that it "rhymes" thoughts not words. This poetry of parallel thoughts keeps its beauty when translated into other languages.

Today, we will begin our own journey into this fascinating, sometimes avoided, and often misunderstood book. In a world that vies for our attention and distracts us from pursuing that which is significant and eternal, Ecclesiastes serves as a heavenly sieve, enabling us to sift out the essential from the nonessential in light of eternity.

Words from the Wise

We're going to come across some interesting words and phrases in the next five weeks, so let's begin by becoming acquainted with them. We'll start with the title, *Ecclesiastes.* It means "Preacher" (sometimes rendered "Teacher"). It finds its roots in the Hebrew word *Qoheleth*, which means "one who calls together an assembly." The Greek translation for the term *assembly* is *ekklesia* and has further been translated to *Ecclesiastes*. So in following the trail of translations, we learn that *Ecclesiastes* refers to the one who calls together an assembly—in other words, *The Preacher.*

We'll gain more insight into the words and phrases below as we travel through the first chapter of Ecclesiastes. Today, we're only going to study the first seven verses, but please read the entire first chapter and count the number of times Solomon uses the word *vanity* (or a form of it), the phrase *grasping for the wind* (*vexation of spirit* in the King James Version), and the phrase *under the sun*, and write down the number of times each of these is mentioned.

Vanity (and any form of it) ________

Under the sun ________

Grasping at the wind (vexation of spirit) ________

As these words and phrases become more familiar over the next five weeks, I believe their significance will begin to take root in your heart, giving you a better perspective of what really matters most in this life we all live, under the sun.

The first chapter of Ecclesiastes really sets the theme for the whole book. Solomon (*The Preacher*) wrote this book in his senior years, dating it at about 940–930 BC. He was older and definitely wiser. He had ruled Israel with more wisdom than any before or after him, yet he had allowed himself to be taken captive by the allure of idolatrous women. Ecclesiastes was written by a man who had it all, took a disastrous detour, strayed from the Living God, and then penned his analysis (under the inspiration of the Holy Spirit) in order to help prevent others from making the same mistakes he had. It's kind of a "Been there, done that, seen that . . . you don't want to go there" kind of story.

In verse 1, Solomon authenticates his authorship. He doesn't have to mention his name. He was the only son of David to ascend the throne, therefore, there may be debate, but I have no real question as to who the author is.

Now let's take a look at some of Solomon's terminology. In verse 2, he uses the term *vanity of vanities* twice. When we find that something is repeated in Scripture it is normally for the sake of emphasis. The double usage here demonstrates his determination to emphasize this phrase, *vanities of vanities*, right out of the starting blocks in chapter 1. Let me give you an example to illustrate the significance of that phrase. You may be familiar with the title *King of kings* given to Jesus. The meaning of that title is that Jesus is the greatest King of all the kings that have ever existed. In the same way, Solomon was saying that this was the greatest of all vanities.

". . . 'Vanity of vanities, all is vanity.'"

Ecclesiastes 1:2

Vanity is an interesting word and can easily be misunderstood, so let's pull out our magnifying glass and get some clarity on its definition. The Amplified Bible says, *"Vapor of vapors and futility of futilities! All is vanity (emptiness, falsity, and vainglory)."* The meaning of these words is "useless, pointless, senseless, temporary, fleeting, or empty." Today, we might say it like this: "Pointlessness of uselessness and emptiness of senselessness! All is fleeting and empty!" Let's just say I don't think Solomon was trying to cheer anyone up.

Is it actually possible for everything to be pointless? Solomon was either the most negative, pessimistic, and depressed person who ever lived, or he was the wisest. The Bible tells us he was the wisest.

The study of Ecclesiastes is certainly not for sissies. It's a hard book with hard truths—but it's definitely a study that has the potential to change our lives. That's why it's important to keep in mind that Solomon's comments come after, and in light of, his own personal experiences, observations, and failures. His years added wisdom, his experience added perspective.

Reflecting on What's Really Important

When we're young, we don't really stop to evaluate life. We're too busy living it to take it too seriously. Solomon was no different. He had lived his life from one extreme to the other, but like a faulty bottle rocket, he started out with a bang for the glory of God but began to fizzle as he was distracted by desire.

Like most of us, as he grew older, he began to carefully examine his life: his frailty, his flaws and failures, his weaknesses and wanderings, his missed opportunities and ultimate accountability. Age tends to resonate with the reality of our own mortality and causes us to take note of the approaching days with a keener awareness of their potential and significance.

In verse 3, Solomon asks a rhetorical question. In your own words, evaluate that question and answer it here.

____

____

____

____

"Do not labor for the food which perishes, but for the food which endures to everlasting life . . ."

John 6:27

Since the fall of man, there's been no such thing as a free lunch (Genesis 3:19). If you want to eat, you have to work . . . it's just a fact of life (2 Thessalonians 3:10). But Solomon is taking us beyond our professions and paychecks; he's talking about the pursuits of our lives, as well: those things that captivate our attention and become the center of our endeavors . . . those dreams in which we invest so much time and that we work so hard to accomplish. Solomon evaluates all our efforts and asks, "What profit is any of it?" Not necessarily what we want to hear, but it's definitely a statement that causes us to evaluate what matters most in light of eternity.

Balance is elusive when our time is spent working for a living, pursuing success, and attempting to live for eternity in the process. Unfortunately, our tendency is to get caught up in the daily grind; to work hard, acquire more stuff, and fit some time in for church once or twice a week. While there is nothing inherently wrong with having a lucrative career and a fat financial portfolio, we are inclined, to lose focus on our eternal perspective in our pursuit of that which is temporary. Perspective helps us understand that if we truly want to make an eternal difference, then we need to have a "forever focus."

A Biblical Perspective on Wealth

📖 Please read 1 Timothy 6:17–19.

Paul tells Timothy to command those who have material wealth not to be __________, nor to put their trust in ______________, but to put their trust in _____ __________________ __________, who gives us richly __________ __________________ to ________________. Let them ______ ______________, so they will be rich in ____________ ____________, ready to ____________, willing to ______________, storing up for themselves a good ________________________ for the time to come, that they may lay hold on ________________________ __________.

Please notice a few things Paul did *not* say. He did not say those who are rich shouldn't have so much in the first place; he did not say they should give up their wealth and take some sort of vow of poverty in order to be "good Christians." He did not rebuke them for being prosperous. He did, however, command them to keep their prosperity in the proper perspective. He was concerned their wealth would produce pride and cause them to lose sight of the Source of their resources. Those who are wealthy need to exercise tight reins on their heart's tendency to be haughty. Paul wanted them to understand that their great financial blessings came with equally great responsibilities. In other words, the wealthy are to have a godly perspective of what God has entrusted to them, and to be a blessing to others in a wise and generous manner. In the end, the stuff we accumulate won't matter; however, what we do for Jesus will.

Everything Changes

📖 Now read Ecclesiastes 1:4–7. Notice the continual motion of things. Nothing stops. The clock keeps ticking regardless of what we do. Recap these verses with me as I paraphrase each one.

Verse 4: One __________dies off and another __________comes into being.

Verse 5: The sun comes ________and the sun goes ________.

Verse 6: The wind blows to the _________ and turns around to the ________.

Verse 7: The rivers run into the ________, yet it is not ________.

Like Solomon, we all come to a point in our lives when we begin to evaluate what really matters most. We begin to think about the brevity of life, realizing there is nothing we can do to stop the process of time. At one time or another, most of us have pondered at least one of the following questions: "What have I done that really makes a difference?" "Does my life really matter?" "What's my purpose?" It's very sobering to know that time is fleeting. It is to that end Solomon wrote Ecclesiastes. At times we need a wake-up call so we can refocus on what really matters most. It is my prayer that, through this in-depth study, we will have a wake-up call to what truly matters most in this life we all live, under the sun.

What have I done that really makes a difference?

I remember a story my husband told me about a surfing trip he took long before we were married. He and some friends traveled to Eleuthera, an island in the Bahamas. One afternoon he turned to one of the locals and asked the time. The man replied, "Time! What is time? The sun goes up and the sun goes down and you do all that you can in between." Well, the real answer to the man's question is, "Time is the stuff life is made of." Yes, the sun goes up and the sun goes down and you do all you can in between, but Solomon reminds us that if we want our lives to amount to more than just a vapor, we need to live life on purpose with an eternal perspective.

Every day we are given choices to live for eternity or to live for the moment. Our clocks don't move backward. We can't recapture time already spent. Oh, how I long to make every moment of this life count! Most likely, it's your desire as well. Please end today's lesson by asking the Lord to help you live each day with an eternal perspective, making an eternal difference with a keen awareness that every tick of the clock is a second you can never relive.

"So teach us to number our days, that we may gain a heart of wisdom."
Psalm 90:12 (NKJV)

Please write your memory verse on a 3x5 card and repeat it three times.

"If then you were raised with Christ seek those things which are above, where Christ is, sitting at the right hand of God. Set your mind on things above, not on things on the earth."

Colossians 3:1, 2

From Vanity to Victory

DAY TWO

AN ENDLESS PURSUIT

Ecclesiastes 1:8–18

My son, DJ, is an extremely talented singer/songwriter and musician, yet he is never satisfied with any of his recordings. Walt Disney was known to have said, "I am never satisfied with my work." As I sit here with my fingers on the keyboard, I'm never satisfied with the way things come out.

Those are simple illustrations, but are we really ever satisfied? We get a new car and it's great until the payment book comes or until we see one we like better. We get a new house and it's not quite big enough, or maybe it's not in the right neighborhood. We're never pretty enough, smart enough, talented enough, successful enough, or popular enough.

Because we live in this flesh, our desires continually long to be filled. Unfortunately, once we get what we want, we are rarely satisfied. I'm reminded of the Veggie Tales DVD *Madame Blueberry,* in which Bob the Tomato is frustrated at Larry the Cucumber's greed for things. He asks Larry, "How much stuff do you need to be happy, anyway?" To which Larry replies, "I don't know. How much stuff is there?"

"Hell and Destruction are never full; So the eyes of man are never satisfied."

Proverbs 27:20

Ecclesiastes 1:8 in the Amplified Bible says, *"All things are weary with toil and all words are feeble; man cannot utter it. The eye is not satisfied with seeing, nor the ear filled with hearing."* We are constantly seeking to find satisfaction with that which cannot give it. Let's face it, we're like a bottomless well. It doesn't matter how much we throw into it, it is impossible to fill it. In fact, we often become weary with what this life has to offer: the drama, the monotony, the hardships, the pointless toiling about in our circumstances and conflicts, the emptiness of the outcome of endless pursuits-chasing the elusive and wondering, "Just how much stuff is there?"

📖 Please read Ecclesiastes 1:9–11. What does the statement, "There is no new thing under the sun" actually mean?

____

____

____

In your opinion, is the heart of man any different today than it was in the days of Solomon? Please explain your answer.

____

____

In the introduction to this book, I stated that times may have changed, but the heart of man has not. No matter how many generations have come and gone throughout the centuries, people are people and they have the same needs and desires regardless of the era or culture in which they live. There is nothing new under the sun.

Biblical and ancient historical figures may be relatively unknown to our twenty-first-century world, but they really weren't much different from you and me. They were real people. They had dreams they pursued just as we do. They desired love, joy, peace, and a long life, just as we do. They fought, they laughed, they joked around; they got mad, jealous, and frightened, just as do all of us. Truly . . . there is nothing new under the sun.

Records have been kept on some who have gone before us, but in reality, we know little or nothing of them. Their lives were important to those they directly affected, but when all is said and done, Solomon was right: *"There is no remembrance of former things, nor will there be any remembrance of things that are to come"* (v. 11).

From verse 12 through verse 18, Solomon tells of his pursuit for human wisdom, human morals, and scientific knowledge. He even became interested in psychology and sociology as he tried to understand what made people tick—why people did the things they did. He concluded that the more he knew, the more frustrated he became.

Solomon set his heart to understand life on an intellectual level. He discovered that knowledge only increased his awareness of how empty life can be. Verse 17 says, *"This also is grasping for the wind."*

I'd like for you to do a little experiment with me. Go stand outside for a moment. Really . . . do it! Now, open your hand and reach out into the air and try to grasp the wind. Now, open your hand and see what you have. Even though I'm not there with you, I can guarantee that you are left empty-handed.

That's what it means to grasp for the wind. Solomon was saying that trying to understand this life with human wisdom or from an intellectual point of view will leave us empty every time. It's all-together vanity.

Pessimistic? Maybe. But I don't think that was his intention. I believe one of his primary purposes in writing Ecclesiastes was so we would understand the gravity of life and be encouraged, even persuaded, to live life on purpose as a result. Knowing the truth of Ecclesiastes 1:9–11 should not minimize the importance of each life—it should cause us to take stock of our journey on Planet Earth and give us a fresh desire to live our life with eternity in view.

So the question is, "If life is so fleeting and passes away, only to be forgotten, how can anything we do really matter at all? What's the point?" The answer is so simple most people miss it. It's this: This life isn't all there is. Ecclesiastes

"But the wisdom that is from above is first pure, then peacable, gentle, willing to yield, full of mercy and good fruits, without partiality and without hypocrisy."

James 3:17

is a blow-by-blow description of Solomon's attempts to make sense out of this life we all live, under the sun—apart from God. He found that a life lived without God and His direction is empty, frustrating, and futile.

I believe that if you're doing this study, you're someone who really wants this life to count. I do, too! So, let's look at what the Bible says about how we can make this life count for more than a vapor . . . for more than grasping for the wind.

To find meaning and purpose, we have to begin at the beginning. In Genesis 1:27, the Bible tells us, *"So God created man in His own image; in the image of God He created him, male and female He created them."* Genesis 2:16, 17 says, *"And the LORD God commanded the man, saying, 'Of every tree of the garden you may freely eat; but of the tree of knowledge of good and evil you shall not eat, for in the day that you eat of it you shall surely die.'"* Genesis 2 goes on to give us the history of the creation of the first woman, Eve.

After God created man and woman and placed them in the Garden of Eden, He told them they could eat from every tree of the garden except from the tree of the knowledge of good and evil. They had the perfect setup. No needs, no worries. Adam didn't even have to break a sweat. Life was *sweet!* God even joined them for a little afternoon walk each day. However, the enemy of our souls was dressed in a serpent's costume one day and he appeared to Eve and began to make her question God. In Genesis 3:1, the Bible tells us, *Now the serpent was more cunning than any beast of the field which the LORD God had made. And he said to the woman, "Has God indeed said, 'You shall not eat of every tree of the garden?'"*

We all know the rest of the story. The serpent sowed doubt in Eve's heart and she began to question God. She ate from the tree and then gave the fruit to her husband to eat as well (Genesis 3:6).

Look back at God's original command regarding the tree of the knowledge of good and evil in Genesis 2:17. What would be their consequence if they were to eat from the tree?

____

____

____

Physical death began its slow and inescapable process (Genesis 5:5). However, the consequence of death meant not only physical death, but spiritual death as well.

Romans 6:23 says, *"For the wages of sin is death . . ."* The paycheck we earn for sin (missing the mark of God's holiness, disobedience to God and His Law) is death. This means physical death, yes, but it also means spiritual death . . . eternal separation from God, ultimately in the lake of fire (Revelation 20:13–15).

The Bible also tells us we are all sinners. Romans 3:23 says, *"For all have sinned and fall short of the glory of God,"* and Romans 5:12 tells us, *"Therefore, just as through one man sin entered the world, and death through sin, and thus death spread to all men, because all sinned."* There is no way around it . . . we are all sinners . . . sinners by nature and sinners by choice. Because of that fact, we all deserve the payment of death, both physically and spiritually.

That leaves us in a mess, doesn't it?! But God loves us so much He provided a way for us to have the relationship He intended for us to have in the first place. He sent His Son, Jesus Christ, to pay the sin debt we owe so we could be forgiven and our relationship with God be restored.

Second Corinthians 5:18 says, *"Now all things are of God, who has reconciled us to Himself through Jesus Christ."* and 2 Corinthians 5:21 tells us, *"For He made Him who knew no sin to be sin for us, that we might become the righteousness of God in Him."* First Peter 3:18 says, *"For Christ also suffered for sins, the just for the unjust, that He might bring us to God."*

God did this because He loves us. John 3:16 tells us, *"For God so loved the world that He gave His only begotten Son, that whoever believes in Him should not perish but have everlasting life."* God loves us and wants us to have an abundant life here on Earth: *"I have come that they may have life, and that they may have it more abundantly"* (John 10:10). And He wants us to have eternal life:*"For the wages of sin is death, but the gift of God is eternal life in Christ Jesus our Lord"* (Romans 6:23, emphasis added).

That's what the cross is all about. It's where payment was made for our sins. But it didn't end there. Romans 4:25 tells us, *"[Jesus] was delivered up because of our offenses, and was raised because of our justification."*

Many of you may be reading this and say, "I believe all this already." But I have to be very honest with you—you can believe all this and still not be saved. James 2:19 says, *"You believe that there is one God. You do well. Even the demons believe—and tremble!"* It's not enough to just believe the facts about Jesus' birth, life, death, and resurrection. The Bible says in John 1:12 we must *receive* Him.

So what does it mean to receive Christ? Well, that's where faith and repentance come in. Faith is believing something to the extent you are willing to surrender your life and follow what you believe. In order to do that, you must be willing to turn from the way you have been living and the things you have been holding on to—in other words, turn from sin and self. Faith and repentance are like two sides of the same coin. You're willing to turn from sin and self and you turn to Jesus and surrender your life to Him, letting Him become Lord of your life. The Bible uses the word *repent* when it speaks of turning. Jesus said in Luke 13:3, *". . . but unless you repent you will all likewise perish."* Acts 3:19 tells us, *"Repent therefore, and be converted, that your sins may be blotted out."*

Faith and repentance are like two sides of the same coin.

If you have ever truly turned from your sins and given your life to Jesus Christ, it will be evident, because at the time of salvation, God changes you. He gives you a new heart, new desires, and a new purpose. Second Corinthians 5:17 says, *"Therefore, if anyone is in Christ, he is a new creation; old things have passed away; behold, all things have become new."*

In John 3:3, Jesus tells Nicodemus, *"Unless one is born again, he cannot see the kingdom of God."* Nicodemus was a very religious leader. He had studied the Scriptures and was well aware Yahweh God had promised to send a Savior.

However, he had to personally realize Jesus was the long-awaited Savior and receive Him into his life. He had to be born again.

We have to have our destination right before our journey can assume a meaningful direction.

We have to have our destination right before our journey can assume a meaningful direction. Our destination is secure when we are born again, and our journey finds significance when we surrender each step of the way to the Lord.

Ecclesiastes is a look at Solomon's attempt to find significance and clarity apart from God in just about everything under the sun. His conclusion? ALL is vanity. Living life apart from God leaves us empty and always looking for the next big thing. Solomon knew it and so do we.

It's like we all have a God-shaped box in our hearts that can only be filled by Jesus Christ. When we give Him our lives and trust Him as Lord and Savior, He fills our hearts with His presence and we finally have the opportunity to make this life count. Remember, this life is not all there is, and if we want to make it count for more than a vapor, we must be born again.

If you've never really surrendered your life to Christ, I implore you to give your life to Jesus today. Start your journey on the only road that leads to eternal life.

Solomon started out well when he asked for wisdom, but he decided to go his own way and search for pleasure and purpose apart from God. His final analysis was that life under the sun, apart from God, is vanity; it is like grasping at the wind . . . you will come up empty-handed every time.

Today, we studied the most important topic this book will cover and that is salvation. Salvation is the starting point . . . it is the road we must take in order to understand what it means to truly live. If you are beginning your faith journey today, I encourage you, first of all, to contact a pastor or a Christian friend and tell them what you have done. They can give you information as to your need for biblical baptism and growing in your walk with the Lord. I'd also like to hear from you. You can e-mail me at eternallyhis@mail.com.

I hope you have already written this week's memory verse on a 3x5 card. If not, please do so today and study it for a few minutes each day. Isn't it such an appropriate verse for what we are learning this week?

"If you were raised with Christ seek those things which are above, where Christ is, sitting at the right hand of God. Set your mind on things above, not on things on the earth." Colossians 3:1, 2

From Vanity to Victory

DAY THREE

ME, MYSELF, AND I

Ecclesiastes 2:1–11

I tend to fly through life with a Burger King mentality. I want it now and I want it my way. Do you? Okay, maybe it's just me, but it seems our tendency to be selfish is something that comes all too naturally. We touched on this unfortunate truth on Day 1, but today we will broaden our scope of study.

As a river flows into the sea, yet is never filled (Ecclesiastes 1:7), so, too, our flesh is continually being fed but is never fully satisfied. In today's lesson, Solomon gives us a vivid account of his attempt to find satisfaction. Maybe Mick Jagger shouldn't feel so bad . . . Solomon couldn't find it, either.

📖 Please read Ecclesiastes 2:1–11 and answer the questions below:
Count the number of times the Bible uses the word I, me, my, mine, or myself and briefly summarize what you think Solomon was saying and whom he was seeking to please.

____

____

____

____

____

____

____

I'm definitely LOL! I can't help but think of how funny these verses sound. *I* did this, *I* did that, so *I* could bring *myself* pleasure. *I* made this for *myself* and *I* became great. Whatever *I* wanted *I* got for myself. Solomon was basically saying, "I made this life all about me!" I'd say he was full of himself, wouldn't you? The essence of pride is the focus on oneself, so I think we could view today's passage as a good description of what pride looks like.

The essence of pride is the focus on oneself.

APPLY Now it's time to take a little look-see in the mirror of your own life (especially the past year) and determine if you've been living a life centered on yourself. Write your reflections here—and be brutally honest.

____

____

____

____

____

____

____

Solomon started out verse 2 by talking to himself, so I think we could assume he was probably going to take us on one of his life's detours down Crazy Street. It actually ended up being a street named "Me, Myself, and I."

"Look out for *Numero Uno.*" "If it feels good, do it." "Life is one big party, so have a good time . . . don't worry about the consequences." We've all heard this world's cry to make this life all about us. Commercials often cater to our love of self in order to push their products, making us think we deserve them. Perhaps you've even bought into it. After all, aren't we worth it?!

People in "developing" countries experience a very different world from ours. They don't just go to the grocery store and buy whatever they want. They take what little money they have and go to the local market and hopefully buy enough to feed their family, even if it's beans and rice for breakfast, lunch, and dinner. Or maybe just enough for one meal a day. They don't just turn on the faucet. Many of them travel miles on foot to polluted water sources only to carry bacteria-infested water back to their villages.

Not only have we allowed ourselves to believe we should indulge ourselves with everything we want, we've been lulled into thinking we must be continually entertained. If you don't believe me, take a look at a list of some of the modes of entertainment on which we spend countless dollars and endless hours . . . then circle the ones you have bought or taken part in.

Television	Movies	Gadgets	Radio
Plays	Dances	Concerts	Magazines
Games	Casinos	Parties	Theme Parks
Skating Rinks	Hand-Held Toys	Bowling Alleys	Sporting Events
Comedy Clubs	Interactive Games	Restaurants w/playgrounds	

Now that's quite a list, isn't it?! Of course, it's not all-inclusive, but it gives us a good idea of our appetite for entertainment. Yet, despite the vast array of forms of entertainment available, we still complain about being bored. Why? Because like a river that flows into the sea, yet the sea in never full, we, too, continually feed this flesh, yet we are never completely satisfied. It seems as though we're always looking for the next big thing.

It seems as though we're always looking for the next big thing.

Unfortunately, our decision to join a local church is often based on what that church has to offer in the way of activities and amusing programs. We sometimes forget we are to follow the leading of the Holy Spirit as He directs us to the church He wants us to be a part of.

In reviewing Solomon's unsavory search for pleasure, let's also do a self-evaluation and see if we are currently attempting to find happiness and contentment in some of the so-called pleasures of this life.

Beginning with Ecclesiastes 2:1, Solomon decides to put a life of pleasure to the test in order to see if he could find happiness in living this life merely for the sake of having a good time. In the last phrase of verse 1, Solomon gives us the outcome of his pleasure test before he even begins to give us his list. He wanted us to know, before we even look at his quite extensive list, he had been there and done that and found it to be vanity.

In verse 2 he declares laughter to be madness and a carefree lifestyle to be futile. In verses 4 through 11, Solomon gives us a rundown of his sordid attempts to find fulfillment.

🕮 Let's begin to look at Solomon's list. Please read Ecclesiastes 2:3. What did Solomon decide to give himself to?

____

Throughout history, many have fallen for the empty promises found in the bottom of a bottle. I've known many who have struggled with alcoholism.

By their own testimony, their personal addiction to alcohol destroyed their marriages, their family relationships, their friendships, and their careers—not to mention their self-respect. In fact, I've never met an alcoholic who could honestly say he or she was happy with his or her life. Happiness is never found in the bottom of a bottle.

Look at the picture Proverbs 23:29–35 (Amplified Bible) paints of how drinking can wreak havoc on the hearts and lives of its victims.

> *"Who has woe? Who has sorrow? Who has strife? Who has complaining? Who has wounds without cause? Who has redness and dimness of eyes? Those who tarry long at the wine, those who go to seek and try mixed wine. Do not look at wine when it is red, when it sparkles in the wineglass, when it goes down smoothly. At last it bites like a serpent and stings like an adder. [Under the influence of wine] your eyes will behold strange things [and loose women] and your mind will utter things turned the wrong way [untrue, incorrect, and petulant]. Yes, you will be [as unsteady] as he who lies down in the midst of the sea, and [as open to disaster] as he who lies upon the top of a mast. You will say, They struck me, but I was not hurt! They beat me [as with a hammer], but I did not feel it! When shall I awake? I will crave and seek more wine again [and escape reality]."*

This isn't about whether it's okay for a Christian to drink. This is about why take the chance on being another sad statistic.

Solomon then tells us of many other pursuits with which he tried to please himself. In verses 4 through 11, we see that Solomon had obtained greater wealth and power than any other king (1 Kings 10:23). He had houses, land, beautiful gardens, vast irrigation systems, servants, concubines, herds, flocks, singers, instruments, gold and silver.

We have to understand that only God and the things of God can fill the spiritual vacuum we all have.

In verse 9, Solomon proclaims his own greatness. Remember, the title of this lesson is, *Me, Myself and I*. Solomon had done all of these things for himself . . . to please himself. In verse 10, he made it clear that he had no restraints. He gratified every craving of his heart. Yet, after he had done pretty much everything possible to fulfill the lusts of his flesh, he tells us in verse 11 that it is all vanity. "It's like grasping at the wind . . . it still leaves me empty." (author's paraphrase).

Why? How in the world can a man have everything his soul desires and still feel as though it is futile? It's because the pursuit for physical pleasure is an attempt to fill a spiritual need. It's like trying to fit a square peg into a round hole. It just won't work. We have to understand that only God and the things of God can fill the spiritual vacuum we all have.

So is it wrong to enjoy the things this life has to offer? Of course not! John 10:10 tells us that Jesus came to give us an abundant life. But, as we learned on Day 1 in 1 Timothy 6:17–19, those who are wealthy are to guard their hearts from the inclination to be self-sufficient and proud. They are told to place their trust in God, to be generous, and to use their financial blessings for eternal purposes. But did you notice the last part of verse 17? It says the rich in this world are to trust in God, who gives us all things richly *to enjoy*. The Amplified Bible says, ". . . who richly and ceaselessly provides us with everything for [our] enjoyment."

Empty is the life that relentlessly pursues to be filled with that which brings only temporary satisfaction and pleasure.

Isn't that awesome?! The God of all creation lavishly and continuously bestows blessings upon us so we can enjoy them. But we have to be careful not to allow the blessings to distract us from the Blesser. Rather than seeking pleasure, we should be seeking God. Empty is the life that relentlessly pursues to be filled with that which brings only temporary satisfaction and pleasure.

Below you will find a personal question. After careful consideration, please answer it honestly.

APPLY Are you seeking a life of pleasure in order to gratify yourself, or are you seeking the Lord of Glory, who can give you real and eternal joy and satisfaction?

(If you're not sure about how to answer this question, think about the things that are important to you, the way you spend your time and your money, what you think about and talk about. These are good indicators of whether you are seeking the Lord or living a life focused on you.)

I'd like to finish today's lesson with a few verses that give us a clear direction as to what we should be pursuing. Please answer the accompanying questions.

Psalm 14:2: What is the Lord looking for?

Psalm 119:2: Who are blessed?

Proverbs 2:1–5: What are we to seek and what will be the result?

Matthew 6:33 – What are we to seek?

📖 Colossians 3:1, 2: What should we be seeking and setting our minds on?

____

____

____

As we conclude today's lesson, I pray we will all be willing to make any adjustments necessary to make the Lord the focus of our lives. After all, it's not all about me, myself, and I . . . It's ALL about JESUS!

Did you notice that the last verse (Colossians 3:1, 2) was our memory verse for the week? Please study it as you keep in mind the lessons we are learning in this study of Ecclesiastes.

"If you were raised with Christ seek those things which are above, where Christ is, sitting at the right hand of God. Set your mind on things above, not on things on the earth." Colossians 3:1, 2

From Vanity to Victory

DAY FOUR

HATING LIFE!

Ecclesiastes 2:12–26

I think I need to prepare you for the very difficult and precarious journey you will be embarking on for the next two days as we tackle the tough topic of depression. These lessons are certainly not for the faint of heart, but they just may help those whose hearts have become faint. Please begin by diving right into Ecclesiastes 2:12–26, and pay close attention to the mood of these verses.

Have you ever heard someone say they hate life? It's a statement that breaks my heart and grieves my soul. Life is a precious gift from God, something to be treasured. Shouldn't Solomon, the wisest man to ever live, have realized that? When someone gets to the point they hate life, they have become a prime candidate for depression.

Life is a precious gift from God, something to be treasured.

Even though I feel as though I'm walking on eggshells, I'm so thankful God's Word addresses this sensitive subject. We will look at the reality of depression in a Christian's life, some of its causes, and the biblical remedy.

I am, by no means, a psychiatrist, psychologist, or even a professional counselor. I do not hold any degrees that would qualify me for giving any clinical evaluations. That's not what these lessons are about. What we will be studying and discussing today is solely based on Scripture and from personal experience. Solomon's not the only one who's walked through circumstances that provoked him to say he hated life.

Living in the United States affords us countless opportunities to live a very comfortable lifestyle in comparison with the rest of the world, yet an estimated 15 million Americans are living with major depression. Think for a moment of your own circle of family, friends, and co-workers. I'm sure you know someone who is either being treated now or has recently been treated for depression.

The *American Heritage Dictionary* defines *depression* as "the condition of feeling sad or despondent. A condition marked by an inability to concentrate, insomnia, and feelings of dejection and hopelessness." After reading Ecclesiastes 2:12–26, we can see that that seems to sum up what Solomon was going through. Solomon was looking at life under the sun and he surmised that whether we choose to live life as a fool or as one who is wise, it didn't really matter because we all die.

Throughout today's text we notice that Solomon kept coming to the same conclusion: "Death is the great equalizer!" When we die, we leave everything we have worked for to someone who, most likely, will not consider it as valuable as we did. That which we skimped, saved, and labored for leaves our homes during an estate sale for next to nothing. If life under the sun is really all there is, then Solomon's state of depression is understandable. But he should have known better!

I have already given you a brief definition of depression, but I'd like to also give you the various types of depression as listed by WebMD:[1]

Major Depression
Chronic Depression (Dysthymia)
Atypical Depression
Bipolar (Manic) Depression
Psychotic Depression
Seasonal Depression (Seasonal Affective Disorder)
Postpartum Depression

Most of these types of depression have similar symptoms and all of them display a feeling of hopelessness or despair. Have you ever felt like that—even for a day or two? When life takes us on a tailspin we all have the propensity to land somewhere between hopelessness and despair. Many people go through a type of depression after the death of a loved one, after being diagnosed with severe illness, after a change in their life, or for no known reason at all. Feeling a sense of depression when our world is turned upside down is a *normal reaction* to those life-altering events. The problem is not *being* in a state of depression—it is *staying* there.

That's what happened to Solomon. Verse 20 in the Amplified Bible says, *"So I turned around and gave my heart up to despair over all the labor of my efforts under the sun."* That actually sums up what happens when someone goes into depression. They give their heart up to despair. It's a choice of the will and of the heart. It's not *what happens* when we respond to difficult situations—it's *where we choose to stay*.

Remember, I am not talking about depression due to a physical cause or chemical imbalance. Nor am I referring to depression as a result of medication or disease. I want to address the reality of emotional depression by giving the true underlying cause of many forms of it, along with its biblical remedy.

Probably the most difficult reality of typical depression is to understand that its root cause is a preoccupation with one's self or one's circumstances. Believe it or not, it is a form of pride. Not pride as we usually think of it, but pride because the focus of our thoughts is continuously on ourselves.

Many times, we go through difficulties with a "Why me?" attitude. We think we should somehow be immune to the hardships of life. I have a friend who had been told she might have a very serious form of cancer. People would make comments such as, "I can't believe you are going through this!" To which she would gently reply, "Why *not* me?" You see, her perspective changed everything. She wasn't thinking about how awful it was that she was dealing with such a grave situation. In her heart and mind, she was thankful she had been healthy for so long, and she understood that sometimes bad things happen to God's people.

📖 Please read John 16:33. What did Jesus say we would have in this world?

____

____

According to this verse, where is our peace?

____

____

Hardships and difficulties are part of this life. There is no vaccination against them. However, Jesus tells us our peace is found in HIM. That means I don't have to be overcome by the overwhelming situations life throws my way. John 16:33 also says we are to be of good cheer. Why? Because He has overcome the world.

John 16:33 also says we are to be of good cheer. Why? Because He has overcome the world.

📖 Please read Romans 8:37 and write it here:

____

____

I wanted you to write the words, *"Yet in all these things we are more than conquerors through Him who loved us."* In all *what* things? The preceding six verses (31 through 36) tell us what things: accusations, guilt, tribulations (life's difficulties), distress (overwhelming circumstances), persecution, famine (hunger), nakedness (poverty), peril, and sword (life-threatening situations).

Dear one, if you have been born again . . . you are a child of God. His Word tells us that in the absolutely worst situations, we are more than conquerors through Him. Don't stay down when the Lord has made you an overcomer. Don't allow fear to hold you captive when Christ has died to set you free. Trust Him. Tell Him you trust Him:

"Although I have no capacity to make sense of the grandness of You, *o*h, Lord, in a world where very little makes sense, trusting You is the only thing that really does make sense! I trust You!"

If the battle with depression is wreaking havoc on your life, you need to know you're not alone. There are many biblical examples of those who have gone through depression. Because of time, I'll only list a few, which you can read at your convenience. Tomorrow, we will learn how to apply a biblical remedy for depression so we can live above our circumstances and help others we know do the same.

Below are a few biblical examples of those who have gone through some type of depression:

Jacob (Israel)

📖 Read Genesis 37:12–36; 45:25–46:1, 29, 30. What was the cause of Jacob's depression?

What words are used to indicate he suffered from depression?

What words are used to describe how Jacob came out of his state of depression?

Job

📖 Read Job 1; 3:1–11; 6:1–3; 10:1–10.

After you have read these verses, write a short paragraph to describe Job's circumstances and his response to them.

David

📖 Read Psalm 22:1–6.

David was so depressed that he felt as though God had forsaken him. Have you ever felt like that? If so, reflect on that time in your life and describe how God helped you see the light at the end of the tunnel.

Asaph

📖 Read Psalm 77:1–4.

Asaph refused to be comforted. He chose to stay in a state of depression. Have you ever done that? If so, briefly reflect on what you were going through and why you chose to stay there.

____

____

____

____

____

____

____

____

____

"I cried out to God with my voice . . ."

Psalm 77:1

MEMORY VERSE

"If you were raised with Christ seek those things which are above, where Christ is, sitting at the right hand of God. Set your mind on things above, not on things on the earth." Colossians 3:1, 2

MEMORY TIP

Make up a tune to go with your verse and sing it to yourself.

From Vanity to Victory

DAY FIVE

Hating Life! (continued)

Ecclesiastes 2:12–26

Yesterday, we talked about depression. We discussed a definition and some of its causes, and we glanced at some biblical examples of the reality of depression in a Christian's life. It's obviously a topic many avoid because it comes with such negative connotations. But it is real . . . it is debilitating . . . it enslaves and renders its victims ineffective.

Now, this is going to be a hard pill to swallow, but it's important to understand that depression skews the perception of reality because it is rooted in self-centeredness, which ultimately clouds our vision from anything else going on around us. Why? Because all we can see are our own circumstances and our own pain. Oh, dear one, if I keep looking in the mirror, all I'm going to see is myself. My flaws . . . my lines . . . my wrinkles . . . my gray hair and my discolored tooth (softball injury :-))—all seem to intensify with each passing moment. That's what depression does. It intensifies our perception of ourselves and our circumstances, leaving little room to see anything else going on in the world around us.

Today, let's begin our lesson by reading Psalm 77:1–9, paying close attention to the way in which Asaph described his feelings. In each verse we see his internal struggle with hopelessness and helplessness. In Ecclesiastes 2:12–26, Solomon described the same kind of hopelessness and despair when he made two very anguished statements: "I hated life" and, "So I gave my heart up to despair."

People who battle depression describe themselves and their circumstances in much the same way Solomon and Asaph did . . . hopeless and helpless. Those two may have lived thousands of years ago, but their words ring true in the heart of every person who is battling depression today.

If you've ever gone through any type of depression, you know it is an internal struggle in which your heart refuses to be comforted. Remember, we can become depressed over any of a number of overwhelming circumstances. That is a normal response to many difficulties in life, but when we refuse to be comforted, we are *choosing* to stay in that state of mind. We hold on to the pain and mince it up over and over again in our minds . . . we can't let it go . . . we won't let it go. Holding on to it becomes like holding a security blanket: It's ours. In many cases, there is a sense of guilt at the mere thought of letting it go. So we choose to refuse to be comforted.

Did you notice I said we *choose?* There's a point we reach when we make a choice about how we are going to respond to any given situation. That's the point in which the normal response time is over, and the choice to stay in depression can take over.

📖 Now read Psalm 77:10–20 and pay close attention to the way in which Asaph begins to shift mental gears.

In verse 10, Asaph seems to make a decision to accept his circumstances. He says, *"And I said, 'This is my anguish.'"* In other words, "This is just how it is for me right now. I'm just going to have to deal with it. It is what it is." But notice that as he goes on, he makes a choice to think in a way that will bring him out of depression. He takes the focus off himself and his situation and chooses to think on some very important aspects of God's character.

Look with me at the process of Asaph's recovery as we walk verse by verse through Psalm 77:10-20. (FYI: I'm using the New King James Version.)

Verse 10a – *"And I said, 'This is my anguish."* Asaph accepts his circumstances. Many times, people stay in depression because at that particular point, life just seems too hard to bear. Asaph came to grips with what he was going through and made an intentional choice to accept where he was in life.

Asaph chose to take his self-absorbed thoughts captive . . .

Verse 10b – *"But I will remember the years of the right hand of the Most High."* Asaph begins this part of the verse with a very important conjunction. Fill in the blanks for the second part of verse 10. *"I will remember the years of the right hand of the Most High."* In the Bible, the term *right hand* refers to "power." With that little word "but" Asaph chose to take his self-absorbed thoughts captive and to remember the many years God had demonstrated His power on behalf of Asaph and the other children of Israel. He realized that no matter what he was going through, God was good, and that he had to bring his thinking into the right perspective. So Asaph chose to remember how God had demonstrated His power on their behalf throughout the years, and he understood that God is God and can do as He pleases.

It's amazing how one little conjunction can change everything. Depression says, "This is just how things are for me right now *and* I hate it." Victory says, "This is just how things are for me right now *but* I will choose to remember how the Lord has been there for me in the past . . . and that will remind me I can trust Him for the future." Do you handle your circumstances with an "and" or a "but"? _____________.

Verse 11 – Asaph chose to remember the ___________ of the Lord and to meditate on His _____________ of old. He continued to choose his thoughts.

Verse 12 – Asaph repeats that he will meditate on God's work. But then he takes it a step further. He begins to verbalize his thoughts. Jesus said, *"For out of the abundance of the heart the mouth speaks"* (Matthew 12:34 NKJV). When we fill our hearts and minds with the goodness and the greatness of God, our thoughts will overflow into the words we say. Our own words can lend healing to our hearts and minds (Proverbs 16:24).

Verses 13 through 15 – In these verses, Asaph meditates on the fact that God is holy (*"Your way, O God,* is *in the sanctuary . . . "*), yet he also realizes God is personally involved in our lives. He has declared His ____________ among the peoples. With His arm, He has _______________ His people.

Asaph may not have been able to grasp the greatness of God, but he found comfort and strength in God's active and abiding presence.

In verses 16 through 19 Asaph reflects on the truth that the earth, the sea, and the sky are completely controlled by God. Then in verse 29 he brings his thoughts back to how personal God is. You can almost hear him say, "God, You are so awesome You control the sea, the sky, and the earth . . . Wow, You are beyond my comprehension . . . and yet, You lead Your people like a flock, using ordinary people such as Moses and Aaron . . . I can trust You to lead me."

"You led Your people like a flock By the hand of Moses and Aaron."

Psalm 77:20

You see, we don't really know when or if Asaph's circumstances ever changed, but we do know that Asaph's way of thinking did, and because he chose to filter his thoughts through the awesome power and love of God, he no longer was held captive to depression.

Job took the first step on his road to recovery when he quit mulling over his own difficult circumstances and quit blaming and questioning God. It was at that point he not only accepted his circumstances, but he also repented of (turned from) his wrong way of thinking (Job 42:1–6). In Job 42:10, something wonderful happened. The King James Version says, "And the LORD turned the captivity of Job, when he prayed for his friends." The New King James Version says, "And the LORD restored all Job's losses when he prayed for his friends."

I don't want you to miss this. Many years ago, I was going through a type of depression. But the Lord showed me this one verse and I began to do exactly what it said. I thought about the Lord and His goodness and then I prayed for the needs of others. Do you see the correlation, dear one? Depression comes from consistently thinking about yourself and your circumstances. What is that called? It's called *pride.* What is pride? It's sin. Job repented of blaming God and thinking only about himself and his situation. He came to the place where he realized he had only been trusting in God's goodness with his head (intellect), but now he was ready to trust God in his circumstances with all his heart. No longer focused on himself and his problems, he positioned his thoughts on how awesome God is. Then he was able to see and pray for the needs of his friends.

When I was going through this very difficult period in my life, my prayers seemed to begin and end with me and my needs, but when the Lord showed me this verse, I repented of my self-centered life and began to pray for my friends. When I did that, the LORD started to lift the fog of depression that had clouded my heart and mind. He restored joy and peace to my life; He set me free from the shackles of depression. That's what He wants to do for you, too.

Remember, Jesus said He came to give us life and to give it to us more abundantly (John 10:10). Rest for our weary and heavy hearts is available when we are willing to come to Jesus (Matthew 11:28).

If you are dealing with depression, you know that you are searching for rest for your weary soul. I want to tell you, dear one, the only way for you to find rest is to run to Jesus, bask in His love for you, delight in His goodness and fix your heart and mind on the greatness of who He is. Like Asaph, your words will then become the overflow of a steadfast heart. With your mind no longer focused on yourself and your circumstances, you can then pray for your friends and, based on God's Word, He will end your captivity and restore you.

I would like to finish today's lesson with a few more practical ways to win the mind battle that causes depression.

📖 Please read 2 Corinthians 10:3–5 and fill in the blanks:
Though we walk in the __________, we do not war according to the __________.

That means we may live in this world, but we don't fight our battles the same way the world does.

What does verse 4 say about the weapons of our warfare?
They are not __________.
They are mighty in ____________.
For the purpose of pulling down ____________.

Make no mistake, the battle begins and ends in the mind . . .

It is important to note that although a *stronghold* is a "place of refuge," it can be used for either good or bad. In other words, if you need a place to go where you can be safe and secure from the battle that rages on around you . . . a stronghold (place of refuge) would be a good place for you to go. However, if the Enemy has a stronghold (place of refuge), that means he has found a safe place to hide. In the negative sense, a stronghold is a place where the Enemy can rest comfortably and take up residence . . . and that is exactly what can happen in the weak areas of our lives. Make no mistake, the battle begins and ends in the mind and the Enemy will penetrate and pillage what we do not protect.

So the question is, How can we guard our minds? Well, the precious Word of God gives us a twofold process.

📖 Please read 2 Corinthians 10:5.
We are to cast down every ____________________ and __________
______ __________ that sets itself up above the knowledge of God.
We are to bring every ___________ ______ captive to the obedience of
_________.

Many people quote this verse without grasping the process of victory over our thought life. Let's look further at what this verse is really saying. We are to deal with every thought that comes into our minds that is contrary to God, to God's Word, to God's character, and to God's ways. The Enemy knows our weaknesses and shoots fiery darts our way in the form of wayward thoughts. He is a liar and a deceiver and since he can't steal our soul, he will try to steal our testimony and our effectiveness.

So if we are diligent to cast down every argument and "high thing" that places itself against the knowledge of God, and if we are careful to bring every thought captive to the obedience of Christ, what exactly should we be thinking about? What does "to the obedience of Christ" really mean? Where should we direct our thoughts?

📖 Please read Philippians 4:6–9. According to verses 6 and 7, we are to be anxious for nothing, but we should be prayerful about everything. When we do this, the ___________ of God, which surpasses all understanding, will guard our __________ and our __________ through ______________.

📖 Now look at verse 8. Notice the arsenal of protective thoughts we are given to guard our hearts and minds:

"But the fruit of the Spirit is love, joy, peace, longsuffering, kindness, goodness, faithfulness,"

Galatians 5:22

True- Jesus is the Truth and all His ways are true.
Noble- Worthy of reverence or honorable
Just- According to God's standards and principles
Pure- Morally clean, undefiled
Lovely- Lovable, friendly, kind, gracious
Of Good Report- Spoken highly of, worthy of respect, courteous
Virtue- Integrity, uprightness, purity
Praiseworthy- Worthy of adoration based on God's standards

Dear one, these are the things we must choose to think on. It truly is a discipline of the mind that can only come from accepting our circumstances, acknowledging God's greatness and goodness in our lives, and then praying for others instead of focusing on ourselves. If you are struggling with depression, I pray that today you will yield to God's practical ways of dealing with our thought life, allowing Him to set you free and give you the rest and peace you so desperately need.

Finish today's lesson by studying your memory verse for the week . . . it's Colossians 3:1, 2.

"If then you were raised with Christ seek those things which are above, where Christ is, sitting at the right hand of God. Set your mind on things above, not on things on the earth." Colossians 3:1, 2

Notes

3

Days of Our Lives

As we walk down the pathway of life, we find that it is paved with a variety of circumstances—some good, some bad. Many times, we have a hard time making sense of it all. In the midst of our meandering we can find hope and comfort in three very important realities:

1. God makes EVERYTHING beautiful in His time.

2. We weren't meant to travel through this life alone.

3. There is an eternity out there where God calls us to join Him.

"These things have I spoken to you, that in Me you may have peace. In the world you will have tribulation; but be of good cheer, I have overcome the world." John 16:33

MEMORY VERSE

"For My thoughts are not your thoughts, nor are your ways My ways, says the L*ORD. 'For as the heavens are higher than the earth, so are My ways higher than your ways, and My thoughts than your thoughts."* Isaiah 55:8, 9

SEASONS OF LIFE

Ecclesiastes 3:1–15

For as long as I can remember, I've been fascinated with theme parks; they are generally my vacation of choice. My plan is to get there as soon as the doors open and stay until they throw me out. I enter the gates, grab a park map, and scurry from one ride to the next. There's a certain strategy to conquering every ride at least twice, you know! The years may have brought my pace down a notch or two, but I enjoy every ride this 40-something body will allow me to ride. Each one is full of ups and downs, twists and turns, catapults and plunges. So, too, is life.

Sometimes it seems like life is a roller coaster of events, taking us to the top, where the view is breathtaking and exhilarating, only to find ourselves plummeting into what seems like certain death, our stomachs turning the entire way down, and just when it looks like we're going to crash—we find ourselves on the way back up again. This journey called *life* can be quite a ride.

We've all experienced those mountaintop moments . . . making a team, hitting a home run, fun times with family and friends, the big wedding day, the birth of a child or grandchild, graduation . . . the list goes on and on. Unfortunately, life isn't always lived on the mountaintop. Pain is also part of our existence: losing a game, failing a course, breaking up with a boyfriend, the death of a loved one, a wayward child, sickness, divorce, injuries, etc. Even as I'm writing this, I can sense the plethora of emotions associated with each event.

God is in control and He makes everything beautiful in His time.

Like a ride on a roller coaster, life is full of unexpected turns and unpredictable ups and downs as we maneuver through the ever-changing seasons of our lives. In Ecclesiastes 3, Solomon encourages us to hang on through each season we face as he reminds us that, although the ride may be rough, God is in control and He makes everything beautiful in His time.

When God spoke the earth into existence, He put into place the laws of nature, which mandate the annual change of seasons (Genesis 1:14). And just as there are seasons and purposes for each season in the natural law of God's creation, there are also seasons and purposes for each season in our individual lives.

📖 Begin today's lesson by carefully reading Ecclesiastes 3:1–10.

You can't help but see the beauty of Solomon's writing in these ten verses. Some give a very clear and simple illustration of the seasons we go through. Others, however, are somewhat obscure in their meaning. The one I found most interesting and probably in need of a little clarity was the first half of verse 5. It says, "A time to cast away stones and a time to gather them together . . ." In order for us to better understand what that means, we need to investigate Jewish culture during Solomon's day.

📖 Please read 2 Kings 3:19 and 25.

What were the stones used for?

Now read Joshua 4:4–7 and Genesis 31:45–50.
What were these stones used for?

After you've read about the Old Testament practice of throwing stones and gathering them, compare what you have learned with Ecclesiastes 3:5.

APPLY Are you headlong in a battle and throwing stones to disable the enemy or are you gathering stones as a testimony to the Lord or as a promise of peace?

Based on the first eight verses of Ecclesiastes 3, what season of your life are you in, and do you have an understanding of the purpose for that season?

Our life is a journey and our pathway leads us through a myriad of seasons. Ecclesiastes 3:1–8 runs the gamut! Some time ago, I was working at a hospital emergency room and a woman came in with her son. She was 42 and her son was two. I remember thinking, *I can't even imagine going through that season of life.* It was so far removed from me. At 43, my boys are 18 and 25. Her season of life included preschool, parks, potty training, and all those other things associated with being a busy wife and the mother of a toddler.

My life, on the other hand, has had a dramatic change of seasons. I was a veteran homeschool mom. Eleven years of attending book fairs, planning curriculum, organizing field trips, teaching at our local homeschool co-op, and—best of all—cherished moments with my children. That, however, has all come to a screeching halt. I've been hurled like a discus into a new season of life and am presently learning how to function to the fullest in it.

Life is ever-changing, yet each new season we face comes with a purpose.

Life is ever-changing, yet each new season we face comes with a purpose. We may not always have a clear understanding of the purpose for the season we are in. However, it would benefit us greatly to recognize and accept the change of each season of our lives, so we don't waste time looking back at what once was. Letting go of the rope of one season is necessary for us to fully take hold of the next one. Sometimes, as difficult as it is, we must realize it is time to move on.

As we continue today's lesson, let's turn our attention to verses 9 through 15. When we read verses 9 and 10, it seems as if Solomon is crying out, "So what's the point?!" Life, under the sun, can be full and exciting, yet at other times it can be painful and wearisome. In the Amplified Bible, Solomon describes the dailies of life as "miserable business." He has just taken us on a roller-coaster ride of seasons and seems to have exhausted himself in the process. But sulking didn't seem to be an option for Solomon.

📖 Please read Ecclesiastes 3:11 and fill in the blanks.
____ has made everything ________________ in _______ time.

God never ceases being God; therefore, He is always in complete control of the ultimate outcome of each event and season of our lives. Solomon understands the character of God and encourages us that, no matter what we go through, God will bring something beautiful out of it.

He takes the ups and downs of our lives, the good, the bad, and the ugly, and He creates a unique work of art.

In Week 1, we looked at the wonderful promise God gives us in Romans 8:28: *"And we know that all things work together for good to those who love God, to those who are the called according to His purpose."* How is it possible that *all* things work together for our good? God weaves together the circumstances of our lives into a beautiful masterpiece. Isaiah 61:3 reads, *"To console them who mourn in Zion, To give them beauty for ashes, The oil of joy for mourning, The garment of praise for the spirit of heaviness . . . "* He takes the ups and downs of our lives, the good, the bad, and the ugly, and He creates a unique work of art. It is important for us to remember that no matter what season we are in, God is the Master Weaver and only He can make something beautiful out of plain (or even ugly) threads of our lives!

📖 Now read the second part of verse 11. Solomon goes on to tell us of our heavenly hope. He says God has put ___________________in our hearts.

God has given us the hope that comes from knowing that this life is not all there is. As we studied last week, He has placed within each of us a God-shaped box, which only Jesus Christ can fill. That is why people of all nations seek to worship something. They are looking for something to fill that void that quietly whispers to each of us there really is an eternity out there where God calls us to join Him.

I remember when God called us to the mission field, He used this verse to remind us that all people of all nations seek to worship something. Our job was to give them a clear picture of who it was their hearts were yearning for.

Verse 11 concludes with the reminder that although we have eternity in each of our hearts, we don't have the capacity to figure God out. His ways are far beyond our ways. So, no matter where you may find yourself or how difficult your circumstances may be today, God will make even that which breaks your heart beautiful in His time. Give God every painful place in your life and let Him give you beauty for those ashes. He will do it, Dear One. His character assures us of that.

Granted, the reality of today's text can leave you weary and discouraged by the ever-changing roller-coaster ride of life. I don't think that was

Solomon's intention at all. Life is exciting and wondrously adventurous, but it is sometimes sprinkled with difficulties, heartaches, and even exasperating boredom. I think that may be why the theme of Ecclesiastes is something such as "Life is short, and death is sure, so make your life count by living for eternity." It's important to remember that the one who lives with an eternal perspective is the one who truly lives.

📖 I'd like for us to conclude today's lesson by reading verses 12 through 15. Paraphrase what you think Solomon is saying in verses 12 and 13.

____

____

____

____

____

"I know that whatever God does, It shall be forever . . ."

Ecclesiastes 3:14

More often than not, we get so caught up in the dailies of life, we don't really enjoy the life we are living. Solomon reminds us to rejoice, to do good, to work for what we get, and to enjoy this life and the things we have, because they are gifts from God. In other words, we need to stop and smell the roses and remember the One who created them.

God loves us and has a wonderful plan for our lives. That plan begins to unfold when we come to Him through receiving Jesus as Lord and Savior of our lives. After that, we can begin our journey with confidence, knowing we are buckled in for the ride of our lives by the very God who spoke this world into being. Rest assured, dear one, we may be in for a bumpy ride at times, but God's hand is still on the controller. God never ceases being God and He has promised, when the ride is over, we will land safely in His loving arms.

Don't forget to review your memory verse for this week.
"For My thoughts are not your thoughts, nor are your ways My ways, says the LORD. *'For as the heavens are higher than the earth, so are My ways higher than your ways, and My thoughts than your thoughts."* Isaiah 55:8, 9

MEMORY TIP
Spend Monday through Wednesday learning the first half of your memory verse and spend the rest of the week learning the last part.

Days of Our Lives

DAY TWO

JUDGMENT DAY

Ecclesiastes 3:16–22

Yesterday, we had the pleasure of learning that no matter what we go through, our ever-present and sovereign God promises not only to be with us, but also to bring beauty out of even the most difficult circumstances. Today, we will tackle the very serious subject of judgment. It's probably one of the most sobering realities of God's Word, but one that needs to be addressed in order for us to live life to its fullest with a clear understanding of what truly matters most.

📖 Begin today's lesson by reading Ecclesiastes 3:16–22 and then answer the following questions:

In verse 16, what did Solomon say was in the place of judgment (justice)?

____

What was in the place of righteousness?

____

If you turn to Psalm 73, you'll find that Asaph had a similar problem. He was troubled by the prosperity and position of the ungodly; he was mystified by the good fortune of the wicked and the arrogant. How could his own life have been riddled with so many trials and tribulations, when he had continually tried to live a devoted and godly life? It just didn't seem fair. At least that's how it appeared under the sun. However, in verse 17 we see that Asaph slipped into the sanctuary and his perspective was drastically changed. It was then he understood the unfortunate fate of the ungodly.

"Until I went into the sanctuary of God; Then I understood their end."

Psalm 73:17

Life isn't always fair, is it? Perhaps Solomon and Asaph aren't the only ones who have a hard time understanding the disparity between the righteous and the reprehensible. In fact, I think we've all looked around at what's going on in this world and thought the same thing at one time or another. A trip to the sanctuary of God's Word will help us come to grips with the many injustices in our world today.

In Ecclesiastes 3:17, what did Solomon say is the fate of all mankind?

____

____

Judgment Day is coming for all of us. It is certain, inescapable. For those who have never been born again, it is a day to be feared. It is a day when everything done in darkness will be brought into the light. Nothing thought to be hidden will escape the eye of God. It is a day when all who have never received Christ will stand before the Lord at the Great White Throne and be judged guilty for every sin they ever committed (Revelation 20:11–15). Their fate will be tragically eternal.

But for those of us who have been saved, it is a day we will stand before the judgment seat of Christ. Now let's not gloss over this important event . . . this is not a place where we will just skip up to the throne and receive crowns for what we've done for the Lord. Scripture teaches us in Romans 14:10–12, 1 Corinthians 3:13–15, and 2 Corinthians 5:9–11 that, although we won't have to be judged for our sins, we will be judged for our works. That's why God's Word constantly reminds us to live soberly, to flee from sin, to set our affections on things above, and to love the Lord our God with all our heart, soul, mind, and strength, and our neighbor as ourselves. Judgment Day is coming!

There is something bittersweet about the Christian's Judgment Day. On the one hand, we will be in heaven . . . we will be accepted by God . . . we will spend eternity with Him . . . we will receive rewards and crowns . . . and, best of all, WE WILL SEE THE SAVIOR! Wait . . . WE ARE REALLY GOING TO SEE THE SAVIOR! The thought of seeing Jesus face-to-face fills our hearts with joy, but it also fills us with sorrow, leaving us to ask ourselves—*What have I done with this life He has given me? How many opportunities did I refuse to take? How often did I fail to obey His call to extend mercy and to love unconditionally? How often did I allow fear to render me useless? How could I possibly ever hear those coveted words,* "Well done, good and faithful servant!"? (Matthew 25:23 NKJV).

As I sit here and write these words I find myself totally incapable of conveying the stark reality and the sheer joy awaiting each and every one of us. I'm desperate for the Lord to give me the words to communicate the urgency to live each day now in light of THAT DAY in the maybe not-too-distant future. You see, on that day, we will truly be engulfed by the unfathomable love of God, for it is at the judgment seat of Christ we will finally understand the extent of what Jesus went through for us on the cross. Our heavenly Father forsook His only Son so we would never have to be forsaken. Jesus took the punishment for our sins . . . He paid our debt and secured our eternity. What a glorious Savior!

> **"Christ has redeemed us from the curse of the law, having become a curse for us . . ."**
>
> **Galatians 3:13**

📖 Please read 2 Corinthians 5:21.
What did Jesus become for us? ______
What do we become because of His willingness to go to the cross?

____

____

WHAT AN EXCHANGE! His righteousness for our sin, His glory for our shame, His hope for our hopelessness, His peace for our torment, His abundant life for our empty life, His power for our weakness, His presence for our loneliness. Right now, we can only get a glimpse of what Jesus accomplished on the cross for us, but on THAT DAY, we will have complete understanding and be overwhelmed by the extent of His sacrificial love.

I can't close the book on this lesson without sensing the overwhelming burden to see you there . . . at the Bema Seat of Christ, where mercy will be extended instead of wrath. That won't happen just because you're reading a Bible study. That won't happen just because you believe in God. It can only happen if you accept what Jesus did on the cross as payment for your sins, place your faith in Him as your Savior, and place your life in His hands as your Lord.

There really is an eternity out there where the Lord invites us to join Him. If you have never truly been born again, I plead with you . . . place your life in His hands . . . trust Him as your Savior. If you do receive Christ during this Bible study, I would love to hear from you. You can e-mail me at eternallyhis@mail.com.

As we conclude today's lesson, I want to take a moment to review what we have learned in the last two days. Solomon started out in Ecclesiastes 3:1–11a with an *earthly reality.* Life is a revolving door of circumstances, which God will make beautiful *in His time.* In Ecclesiastes 3:11b–15, Solomon reminds us we are here for more than a ride. He tells us of an *eternal hope* placed in each of us, and our focus is to be . . . on eternity. Finally, in Ecclesiastes 3:16–21 he points us to our *eminent destiny.* In these verses, he not only encourages us to have a proper perspective of the apparent injustices of this world, he also reminds us we will all give an account for the choices we make and the things we do in this life we all live, under the sun.

I pray we will all live each day with a proper perspective of our earthly reality, motivated by our eternal hope and in light of our eminent destiny. Having this "forever mindset" will enable us to live the abundant life the Lord desires for each of us.

MEMORY VERSE
"For My thoughts are not your thoughts, nor are your ways My ways, says the LORD. *'For as the heavens are higher than the earth, so are My ways higher than your ways, and My thoughts than your thoughts."* Isaiah 55:8, 9

MEMORY TIP
Write your memory verse on a 3x5 card and tape it by your kitchen sink. Study it while you're doing the dishes.

Days of Our Lives

DAY THREE

DOING A DOUBLE TAKE

Ecclesiastes 4:1–8

We do it all the time. We see something strange and we do a double take to be sure we actually saw what we thought we saw. I remember that when we lived in Costa Rica we were driving to the airport one day and looked over to the right, where we saw a group of people gathered around the body of a young man who had just fallen off a cliff to his death. It was so surreal. There was a gated median between us and the man, so we weren't able to stop and offer assistance, but as we drove away, we just kept looking back, wondering if what we had just seen was real.

In Ecclesiastes 4:1–8 Solomon appears to be doing a double take at three specific aspects of life, as if to say, "Can these things really be?" Let's consider his observations and see what we can learn from them.

". . . In the place of judgment, Wickedness was there . . ."

Ecclesiastes 3:16

📖 Please read Ecclesiastes 4:1–3 and describe what you believe Solomon is saying.

____

____

____

📖 Now look back at Ecclesiastes 3:16, 17 and describe what you believe Solomon is saying.

____

____

____

Looking Back at Injustice
If you've ever seen the movie *The Lion King,* you might remember the scene where Mufasa told Simba to "look closer."[2] Well, that's exactly what

Solomon is doing: looking closer. In Ecclesiastes 3:16, 17 he glances at the reality of oppression and injustice as a whole and seems to find solace in the fact Judgment Day is coming. It's almost as if he is warning the wicked and comforting the just with the same words: "Judgment Day is coming." To the wicked, "You'll get what you deserve, buddy." To the just, "He'll get what he deserves and God will vindicate you." In today's verses, Solomon's deliberate examination led to an expanded view of oppression. No longer was it something he saw from a distance . . . it was a real problem that brought pain and heartache to real people.

Throughout history, many of the atrocities of social and political injustice have been recorded for us to read. Our hearts have been broken by some of the brutalities that have gone on before and, yes, during our time. But reading about it and seeing it on television only expose us to a small fraction of the reality of the victims' pain.

In the United States, we really don't have a clear understanding of what persecution and oppression are. To *oppress* someone means "to exercise authority or power in a burdensome, cruel, or unjust manner." To *persecute* means "to afflict, torment, or torture, specifically because of race, religion, or beliefs." The Middle English origin of the word "persecute" comes from the idea of pursuing intently. It carries the thought of one who is pursing someone else with intent to harm or harass.

That type of behavior is exactly what Solomon is talking about in Ecclesiastes 4:1–3. It is also something the United States hasn't experienced for about one hundred fifty years. The horrors of true oppression were felt by the slaves for more than two hundred years in America. They were beaten, raped, tortured and killed. Children were taken from their parents, husbands and wives were taken from each other. The slaves had no rights, no voice, and no comforter. As undeniably appalling as it sounds, this is a snapshot of our country's history. This is true oppression.

Today, as you are reading this book, millions of people are still experiencing the realities of this type of treatment. People in North Vietnam, Sudan, Somalia, Eritrea, Saudi Arabia, China, Iraq, Iran, and countless other countries suffer the day-to-day realities of ruthless tyranny. In fact, the organization *Voice of the Martyrs* is documented to currently be working with more than forty 40 countries, where oppression and persecution of Christians is known to be occurring.[3] In many countries it is a way of life—for Christians and non-Christians alike. It is real . . . it is painful . . . it is tragic.

> ***"At my first defense no one stood with me, but all forsook me . . ."***
>
> ***2 Timothy 4:16***

Look with me at Ecclesiastes 4:1 from the Amplified Bible:

> *"THEN I returned and considered all the oppressions that are practiced under the sun: And I beheld the tears of the oppressed and they had no comforter; and on the side of their oppressors was power, but they [too] had no comforter."*

Neither the oppressed *nor* the oppressor had a comforter.

It is understandable the oppressed would need to be comforted; however, it is incomprehensible to think the oppressor would need the same. Those who have experienced the cruelty of oppression are desperate for comfort for their broken hearts and lives. However, those who perpetrate such atrocities are in need of comfort for an empty heart that has become laden with bitterness, guilt, and shame. Yes, many may have begun their brutal behavior because of a ruthlessly depraved heart, but that doesn't minimize their emptiness, nor does it eradicate the escalating weight of guilt and shame that plague those who commit such acts. Yet, according to Solomon, neither had a comforter.

Remember, Solomon's perspective was only one-dimensional—he was only looking at life under the sun, so his observations fell short of God's promised provision of a Comforter. Jesus promised He would not leave us comfortless, but that He would send us another Comforter (John 14:16, 17, 26 KJV). In the New American Standard Bible, we find the word *Helper.* The original Greek word is *Parakletos*, which means "Intercessor, Consoler, Advocate, Comforter." That is exactly who the Holy Spirit is for those of us who have been born again. He comes alongside us and encourages us, He strengthens us, He assists us in our time of need. He is our Intercessor, our Consoler, our Advocate, and our Comforter.

📖 Look at this precious promise from God found in Romans 8:26, 27:

> *"Likewise the Spirit also helps in our weaknesses. For we do not know what we should pray for as we ought, but the Spirit Himself makes intercession for us with groanings which cannot be uttered. Now He who searches the hearts knows what the mind of the Spirit is, because He makes intercession for the saints according to the will of God."*

It is truly comforting to know, whether we are facing persecution and oppression or some other tumultuous trial in our life, we have the promised Comforter, not only to help us during our time of need, but also to pray for us when words elude us.

Looking Back at Motives for Success

📖 As we continue in today's lesson, we turn our attention to Ecclesiastes 4:4. What does Solomon say is the motive for all of man's hard work?

____

📖 According to Proverbs 14:30, what is the consequence of an envious heart?

____

📖 Please read 1 John 4:7, 8. According to these verses, what is to be a prevailing characteristic of one who is born again?

____

____

Envy has a way of clogging the drain of love that should be flowing from our lives.

📖 Now please read 1 Corinthians 13:4 and fill in the blanks.
Love is _____________ love is __________, love is not ________, love does not ___________, love is not ___________.

Envy has a way of clogging the drain of love that should be flowing from our lives. What backs up in the sink of an envious heart is never a pretty sight.

Take a moment to think about your own life and ask the Lord to reveal to you if you have harbored a heart of envy against someone else. If you have, ask the Lord to help you employ His principle of putting off and putting on (Ephesians 4:22–24); in this case it would mean to put off envy and put on love.

Looking Back and Finding Balance

Recently, I went with my friend Dawn to watch her daughter's gymnastics competition. I was fascinated by the events on the balance beam. It's only four inches wide. I just measured and my foot is four inches wide! That's all the room they have to do flips, jumps, cartwheels, backbends, and walk-overs. It definitely takes a lot of dedication and a lot of concentration to even walk on that thing, let alone do flips!

Balancing our lives is very much like walking on a balance beam: Leaning too far in one direction will land us on the mat. We all know it's not easy. We're women, wives, mothers, daughters, employees or employers, and friends. We all have a lot on our plates. That's why it's so important to live a life of balance. It requires the same dedication and the same level of concentration to balance our lives as it does to compete on the balance beam. Let's face it, we're all walking on the balance beam of life and there are times when we just lean too far in one direction or another.

Solomon deals with the issue of "being balanced" in Ecclesiastes 4:5–8 as he shows us the self-destruction brought on by one's own slothfulness (v. 5), the blessing of a balanced life (v. 6), and the calamity of the compulsive worker (v. 8).

📖 Look at Ecclesiastes 4:5. Explain what you think this verse means.

____

____

____

Indolence ruins potential and self-respect. Laziness bears a barren tree. It produces nothing for itself or anyone else. The Bible tells us in 2 Thessalonians 3:10 that if a man does not work, then he shouldn't eat. Throughout the book of Proverbs, Solomon condemns laziness (Proverbs 10:4; 13:4; 19:15, 24; 20:4; 21:25), yet his description of the relentless laborer's life wasn't any better (Ecclesiastes 2:17–23).

"The soul of a lazy man desires, and has nothing . . ."

Proverbs 13:4

Most workaholics tend to justify their consuming work schedules, but no excuse can compensate for what they lose in the process. How in the world can you enjoy the "stuff" you accumulate if you are working eighty hours a week to do so? What good is a big house if sleeping is the only thing you have time to do there? And truly, at the end of our lives, we will wish we had spent more time with those we love. No one approaching death laments, "I wish I had spent more time at work."

It won't matter how big our house is then, nor will it matter what kind of car we drove, how much jewelry we had, or if we wore the latest styles. However, it *will* matter what we did for Jesus . . . it *will* matter if we poured our lives into others . . . it *will* matter if we pointed others to the Lord. Solomon is desperately trying to tell us to quit putting all our eggs in this earthly basket and to live life with an eternal perspective.

In Ecclesiastes 4:6, Solomon gives us a balanced approach to life. It wasn't easy for him to live a balanced life and it isn't easy for us. The demands of life are constantly pulling us in one direction or another. Finding balance in the midst of our chaos sometimes calls for us to analyze our priorities. I'm a girl who readily confesses the need for a periodic priority check. If I don't take time evaluate how I've been stacking the plates of my life, I find myself picking up the pieces, instead.

Let's look at some biblical examples of people who had their priorities out of whack.

David should have been on the battlefield with his troops. Instead he was sneaking a peek at Bathsheba from his rooftop (2 Samuel 11). That peek led to adultery . . . and that adultery led to murder. When our priorities aren't right, we make ourselves vulnerable to sin—sin that defeats us and is often detrimental to others. Keeping our priorities in line keeps *us* in line, as well.

When our priorities aren't right, we make ourselves vulnerable to sin—

Abram (later named Abraham) was more worried about protecting himself than he was about protecting his wife, Sarah, and his integrity. (Genesis 12). Asking his abliging wife to lie to Pharoah and say she was Abram's sister may have saved his skin, but it also put Sarah in danger. Her honor, her virtue, and her life were at stake the minute she mislead Pharoah. Abram's sin brought serious repercussions, not only for Sarah, but also for Pharaoh's household. Ultimately, because Abraham's priorities were flawed, his testimony became flawed . . . not only in the sight of Pharaoh, but in Sarah's heart, as well. When our priorities are awry, our vision is often distorted and our integrity is compromised. Keeping our priorities in view helps others have a positive view of us.

Rebecca knew that God had promised the inheritance to Jacob, but when it was time for Isaac to dole out the blessings, she thought she'd be God's little helper. After concocting a deceptive course of action, Rebecca convinced Jacob to masquerade in a mohair suit and disguise himself as Esau. Betrayed by his second born son, Isaac granted Jacob the blessing reserved for his first born son, Esau. (Genesis 27). In the process of securing Jacob's blessing, Rebecca not only told her son to lie, but she actually *taught* her son to lie. When we lose sight of our priorities, we lose sight of God's ability to work ALL things together for our good, and we begin to doubt His faithfulness. Keeping our priorities in view helps us keep God's power and presence in view.

Today's study has been an adventure in Solomon's reflections. I pray his double take will become more than fodder for our future, but that it will foster change. Remember, the easiest lessons to learn are someone else's.

First, he looked at the reality and the results of oppression. May this lesson begin to spark a level of interest in your heart that would prompt you to pray for those who are oppressed today. I also pray that it will be a sweet reminder that we are not left comfortless. We have been given the Holy Spirit to help us in our time of need. He even prays for us when life leaves us speechless.

Second, I hope you will be encouraged to live a balanced life. Give yourself a little priority check every now and then. Do whatever you is necessary to readjust, realign and reposition your life so that you can reaffirm and refocus on what matters most.

I'd love to help you get started by taking a little priority test. Take a minute to reflect on your own life and make a list of your priorities over the past three months. (Remember: The way you spend your time is generally indicative of what is important to you.) Then make a list of what you know your priorities *should* be. When you are done, ask the Lord to help you adjust your priorities.

My Priorities Now	What My Priorities Should Be
____________________	____________________
____________________	____________________
____________________	____________________
____________________	____________________
____________________	____________________
____________________	____________________

Don't forget to study your memory verse and ask the Lord, "Whose ways are so much higher than ours?" to give you the wisdom and determination to live a balanced life. Remember . . . He has given you the Comforter to help you.

"For My thoughts are not your thoughts, nor are your ways My ways, says the Lord. *'For as the heavens are higher than the earth, so are My ways higher than your ways, and My thoughts than your thoughts."* Isaiah 55:8–9

MEMORY TIP
At dinnertime, write your verse on a 3x5 card and pass it around the table once. Have each person read it out loud. Then go around the table and see who can say it without looking at the card. Everyone will be memorizing God's Word!

Days of Our Lives

DAY FOUR

You've Got a Friend

Ecclesiastes 4:9–12

Yesterday, we reflected on broken hearts, battered lives, being balanced and our caring Comforter. Today, we will be heading in an entirely different direction as we turn our attention to the topic of friendship.

Okay, girls, I have to admit I am very excited about today's lesson because the Lord has blessed me beyond measure with several good, godly friends. They are living descriptions and definitions of the word *friend.* Unfortunately, their lives often remind me of how far I fall short of being not only the kind of friend they deserve, but also the kind of friend the Bible calls me to be.

Friends are powerful influences in our lives.

Friends are powerful influences in our lives. They have the capacity to encourage us to live as we know we ought and to challenge us to accomplish more than we could envision. Yet, they are also capable of dragging us lower than we thought we'd ever go and into doing things we thought we'd never do. That's why it is so important we choose our friends wisely. The

Amplified Bible tells us in Proverbs 12:26, *"The [consistently] righteous man is a guide to his neighbor, but the way of the wicked causes others to go astray."*

📖 Begin by reading today's Scripture passage, Ecclesiastes 4:9–12.

It is interesting to note that many theologians believe that Solomon's illustrations mimicked two people walking along a trail together. What a wonderful parallel to our own life's journey! This pilgrimage we call *life* often takes us down some interesting and difficult roads. Life can be hard, but we weren't meant to make the trek alone. We need friends!

I am reminded of an "oldie but goodie" song, "You've Got a Friend,"[4] performed by James Taylor and written by Carole King. You can Google the lyrics to this song if you like, then sit back and reminisce about your own friendships as you read through each line of this song. It is really good to know that we've got a friend!

If you are like me, you were singing the song by the time you were halfway through the lyrics. We all need to know there is someone we can trust, someone we can laugh and cry with, someone we can turn to in time of need. Do you have a friend like that? Are you that kind of friend?

Based on our Scripture passage for today, let's look at four aspects of friendship.

"Two are better than one, Because they have a good reward for their labor."
Ecclesiastes 4:9

1) First we will look at the benefits of *working together.*

📖 Please read Ecclesiastes 4:9, where Solomon tells us two are better than one because there is a more satisfying reward when they work together.

APPLY Think of a time you worked with a friend to accomplish something and how you felt after you were done. Write your reflections here.

____

____

____

____

____

Why do you think it was more rewarding to accomplish it together?

____

____

____

____

Black Friday is an extreme shopping day for women everywhere and it's when my friend, Dawn, and I escape for our annual Christmas shopping extravaganza. Both of us hate to shop, but it's a necessary evil. At 4:30 in the morning we find ourselves in the van, drinking coffee and laughing at each other for getting up so early to do something neither of us enjoys. Yet, together, it's fun and rewarding. It's fun because we are together and we both realize "real shoppers" wouldn't be able to put up with either of us for a minute. It's rewarding because we're able to find those after-Thanksgiving deals and save a lot of money in the process.

Working together gives a sense of joint accomplishment while it solidifies friendships and creates a lifetime of sweet memories. The "reward for their labor" Solomon mentioned is not only the finished product but the joy of the journey together. Two really are better than one!

2) In Ecclesiastes 4:10 we see the benefits of *helping each other in time of need.*

Remember, Solomon's description is most likely in reference to friends taking a journey together. The roads of Solomon's day were not neatly smoothed and paved. In fact, they remind me of a Costa Rican road; potholes you could lose your car in, gullies that look more like rivers, narrow passages on steep mountains, and scattered debris . . . not to mention those who stealthily lurk behind the bushes awaiting their next victim.

"For if they fall, one will lift up his companion . . ."
Ecclesiastes 4:10

It would be difficult for me to overemphasize the need we all have for friends on this pathway called *life.* We may think we are able to handle things on our own, but when we fall we need someone who cares enough to stop, reach down, and lift us out of the mess we're in. I may stumble over my own messy decisions, but when I do, I don't need people to pass by and gawk at me, I need help—I need a friend. And so do you.

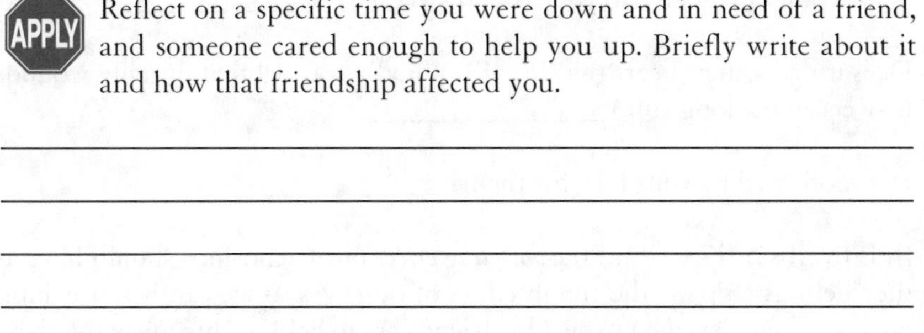

Reflect on a specific time you were down and in need of a friend, and someone cared enough to help you up. Briefly write about it and how that friendship affected you.

When we lived in Costa Rica, I had some health issues and needed to travel back to the States to have surgery. Donald had some things to take care of so he wasn't able to fly with me. My son, DJ, was the strong shoulder I leaned on during the trip. He encouraged me and took care of me the whole way. When I arrived weak and pale, my friend was there waiting for me at the airport. She had driven 180 miles to pick me up, and on the way home we had to make an all-night pit stop at an emergency room. She was there for me before and after the surgery: helping me to the bathroom, caring for me, scolding the nurses when she thought they weren't attentive enough. What a pal! What a friend! I was down and she lifted me up. Her unfailing friendship has taught me what it means to be a friend. She has truly been the Proverbs 17:17 friend who has loved me at all times.

3) As we continue today's lesson, we find some snuggling going on in Ecclesiastes 4:11. It's a picture of two friends keeping each other warm on a cold night. This verse teaches us that warmth may be transferred physically, but it also suggests *we should bring warmth to each other's character.* I remember one night, when I was working at the hospital, I responded rudely to a friend. She waited a few minutes and then came and gently rebuked me. She was right and I was thankful she was willing to straighten me out!

As I reflect on one of the character traits of a good, godly friend, I'm reminded that being a good friend doesn't mean we only say what she *wants* to hear . . . it means we are willing to say what she *needs* to hear. Being a good friend means we are able to give and receive godly counsel. It means we help tone each other down when necessary, and bring out the best in each other.

Being a good friend doesn't mean we only say what she wants to hear.

📖 Please read Proverbs 27:6, 9, and 17 and answer the following questions.

APPLY Reflect on a time when you have either been wounded by the counsel of a friend or when you have had to give advice you knew would be painful for your friend to receive (Proverbs 27:6). Are you willing to receive godly counsel—even when it hurts?

When we give counsel to our friends, it should be based on God's Word and should stem from a heart of love for them, not from anger, pride, or selfishness (Proverbs 27:9).

Is the counsel you give to your friend sweet? ______________

Does it make their heart rejoice? (Even godly counsel that initially wounds is sweet in the long run.) ______________

Is it motivated by your love for them? ______________

In Proverbs 27:17 we find the *chiseling effect* our friendships should have as they help us chip off the rough edges of our lives so we can better exhibit what we were designed to be. Our friends are to help us chip away the characteristics that make us dull and unable to reach our fullest potential. We're to sharpen one another and assist in making each other fit for use.

APPLY Think for a moment about your friendships. Whom are you sharpening?

Whom are you allowing to sharpen you?

4) In Ecclesiastes 4:12 we see the *need for an ally* as we are reminded we have an adversary who lies in wait to attack us when we least expect it and when we're at our most vulnerable. When we have a friend in whom we can confide, one who will help us fight our battles, then we are much less likely to lose the fight.

APPLY Take a moment and describe a time a friend helped you ward off an attack during a time of trial and/or temptation.

____

____

____

____

____

We conclude today's lesson with the last part of Ecclesiastes 4:12: *"A threefold cord is not quickly broken"* (KJV). Many scholars believe the transition from *"two are better than one"* to *"a threefold cord"* is a reference to the inclusion of Jesus in all our friendships. Other scholars believe it is a reference to more than two friends. Whichever is the correct intent of verse 12, both are true.

We all need more than one friend. They all minister to us at different times and in different ways. It is also true that Jesus should be the foundation of our friendships. Yes, we need each other, but more than that . . . we need Jesus! If we are to lift each other up in time of need, reap the benefits of working together, encourage one another, sharpen one another, bring warmth to each other's character, and strengthen one another as we fight our battles, then we need Jesus, don't we?!

Jesus should be the foundation of our friendships.

I learned a long time ago it's impossible to be the kind of friend I need to be without relying on the Lord. I tend to be selfish and get so caught up in life's daily grind I'm often blinded to the needs of my friends. I need the Lord's wisdom and prompting to direct me to be the kind of friend I should be. I need His strength, His humility, and His love to flow from my life into the lives of those around me. My friendships are strengthened beyond measure by the presence of the Lord . . . and so are yours.

Today, we've had the privilege of studying some of the characteristics of friendship. I pray that you were encouraged by the sweet memories of your own friendships and also challenged to be the kind of friend you know you should be. I also pray that you were reminded to let Jesus be the foundation of all your friendships.

It is my deepest desire that you know that no matter what you may be going through, no matter how far you may have fallen, no matter how rough your edges are, no matter how strong your storm is, you've got a friend who sticks closer to you than a brother. His name is Jesus Christ. He will never leave you; He will never forsake you. He will not allow anything to separate you from His love. He will pick you up, He will bring warmth to your character, He will fight your battles—and He enjoys spending time with you. You are the apple of His eye and He loves you with an everlasting love.

Ain't it good to know . . . you've got a Friend!

As you study your memory verse, reflect on the truth that though His ways are so much higher than ours, He has chosen us and He calls us friends (John 15:15, 16). What a wonderful Savior, what a wonderful Lord!

"For My thoughts are not your thoughts, nor are your ways My ways, says the LORD*. 'For as the heavens are higher than the earth, so are My ways higher than your ways, and My thoughts than your thoughts."* Isaiah 55:8, 9

Days of Our Lives

DAY FIVE

THE OXYMORA OF LIFE

Ecclesiastes 4:13–16

Have you ever said something that made absolutely no sense at all? I tend to do that quite frequently, cracking myself up in the process. An *oxymoron* is a "contradictory group of words or a concept that just doesn't make sense." I've listed a few for your reading pleasure. As Momma used to say, you're going to have to put your thinking cap on, but take a minute and think about how these phrases make absolutely no sense at all. Allow yourself to LOL as you read them out loud.

Absolutely unsure	Friendly argument	Home office
Modern history	Paid volunteer	Farewell reception
Organized mess	Original copy	Bad health
Working vacation	Virtual reality	Modern classic

Why do people call evil good and good evil?

The list above may have made us LOL, but oftentimes the oxymora (I know it sounds funny, but it's right) of life are nothing to laugh at. Many times we see unfair and even tragic circumstances as we stand back and just shake our heads. We wonder why evil seems to prevail over good. Why is it that the unrighteous seem to climb to political popularity while the righteous are mocked? Why do people call evil good and good evil? Why is it that violent criminals get off with light sentences, while petty thieves seem to get the book thrown at them? In today's text Solomon describes the unfortunate fate of two men and we will learn that some things just don't make sense.

📖 Please read Ecclesiastes 4:13–16, filling in the blanks below and answering the questions.

The youth of the story is ________________ and ____________.
He came out of ____________________ and became a ________________.
The old king is described as being ______________.
What was the fate of the old king? ______________.

Verses 15 and 16 depict the new king's fan club. How long did his popularity last?

____

____

Solomon concludes that this, too, is vanity, a grasping for the wind. Under the sun, it may be better to be wise in this life . . . to pull yourself up by your bootstraps and live life to the fullest as did the poor, wise youth. But in the end, the applause fades into animosity. The revered becomes the rejected. The famous becomes the forgotten.

As I was reading these verses, I was reminded of Joseph of the Old Testament.

📖 To get a better understanding of the correlation between the two, please read Genesis 37:23–36. What did Joseph's brothers do with him (verses 27 and 28)?

____

____

____

____

What did they tell their father (verses 31 and 32)?

____

____

Where did Joseph end up (verse 36)?

____

____

____

📖 Now read Genesis 39:1–5, 7, 8, 11–23. Summarize what happened to Joseph.

____

____

____

____

Look carefully at verses 2 through 5 and 21 through 23, then describe what kind of reputation Joseph had and why.

____

____

____

____

Shackles may have limited Joseph's freedom but they also revealed his character.

Shackles may have limited Joseph's freedom but they also revealed his character. It wasn't long before Potiphar noticed that Joseph was not only a man to be admired, but a man to be trusted, as well. He was given a position second only to Potiphar's, but more importantly, his life gave evidence of the power and presence of God. Joseph's life was blessed by God and, as a result, his blessings overflowed into the lives of those around him. His big mouth may have caused his brothers to throw him in a pit, but his character prompted his position and power.

APPLY Think for a moment about your own life and answer the following questions:

When I'm facing difficult circumstances, do I behave in a way that causes others to see God's hand in my life? Explain your answer using your response to a recent event as an example.

____

____

____

____

____

____

____

Just as did the poor, wise youth in Ecclesiastes 4, Joseph defied all odds. Neither man allowed his circumstances to define his character. Instead, both used their circumstances to display their character.

We're going to discover three very good and practical life lessons in today's Bible readings.

1. *Don't judge a book by its cover.* The king was older and should have been wiser for his years. His own life experiences should have taught him the value of listening to wise counsel. However, he chose to ignore them. The Amplified Bible says he no longer knew "how to receive counsel" (Ecclesiastes 4:13). In contrast, we normally think of the younger generation as impetuous and lacking in wisdom.

We judge by what we see, but God sees straight to the heart.

Both the old king and the young man teach us we should never judge a book by its cover. Unfortunately, we tend to do exactly that. We judge by what we see, but God sees straight to the heart. He is not a respecter of persons. Outward appearances are so deceiving, yet we are easily impressed by the popular, the affluent, and the powerful. There is latent potential in many whom society deems outcasts. May we look for the best in others and take every opportunity to help others see the best in themselves.

In our previous church, we worked with an awesome group of college and career students. What a huge pool of potential! Theirs is an awkward age because it's a time of transition, overflowing with new responsibilities, new possibilities, and limitless questions. *What am I going to do? Should I go to college? What college? What should I study? What kind of job do I want? Do you mean I have to pay that bill? Should I date him? Should I marry him?*

These precious young people always made my heart smile because I saw them not only for where they were, but also for where they could be. They're a tough group to minister to because they have so much going on in their lives, but what a wonderful chance to help them see the potential that lies beneath, just waiting to be revealed at the perfect time! Oh, Dear One, it's so important we don't judge a book by its cover.

2. Persevere through adversity. Joseph's life paints a painful but courageous picture of what it means to persevere through adversity. Envied and betrayed by his brothers, Joseph was plunged into a pit and then sold into slavery. In the midst of his mayhem he managed to maintain his integrity and work his way up to second in command. Enraged by Joseph's lack of response to her flirtatious behavior, Potiphar's wife falsely accused him of attempted rape. He then spent another two or so years in prison before divine intervention combined with divine interpretation became the key that unlocked his dungeon door.

In each circumstance, he didn't just endure, he persevered. His behavior captivated the attention of his masters and he turned a seemingly hopeless situation into a satisfying and successful one.

📖 Please read Romans 8:28.

How many things work together for our good? __________
Do you believe that? __________

Joseph's life proved *he* believed it. Our lives should prove we believe it, too.

3. Make this life count by making an eternal difference in the lives of others. Solomon realized fame is fleeting. That was true in his day, that was true in Jesus' day, and it remains true today. You may remember reading Mark 11:1–11, which describes Jesus riding into Jerusalem on a donkey and the people spreading their garments and palm branches out in front of him as they cry out, *"Hosanna! BLESSED IS HE WHO COMES IN THE NAME OF THE LORD; Blessed is the coming kingdom of our father David; Hosanna in the highest!"* Just days later, the multitude was crying out, *"Crucify Him! . . . Crucify Him!"* (Mark 15:12–14). Fame is truly fleeting, but the impact we can have in the lives of others has the potential to last throughout all eternity.

Make this life count by making an eternal difference in the lives of others.

No matter who you are or where you come from, you have been uniquely created *by* God and *for* God. He has placed opportunities before each of us and we have all been given a sphere of influence in which we are to make a difference. That takes time and effort. It means we have to step outside our own lives long enough to look for ways to minister to others. Living an intentional life can make an eternal difference.

You probably have heard the expression, "They don't care how much you know until they know how much you care." As missionaries, we have worked with many different groups of people. Most of them are poor beyond our North American understanding. We know it's hard for them to listen when their bellies are growling. We also understand we earn a listening ear when we meet a physical need. When others see the love of Jesus in action, it will cause them to want to hear about it.

Making a difference in the lives of others means loving them as Jesus does . . . sacrificially. It means showing them that Jesus is real by living what you believe. In fact, today, ask the Lord to help you make a difference in the life of someone who needs to see His love in action. Write that person's name on the palm of your hand. I know that sounds strange, but we are inscribed on the palm of God's hand, meaning we are constantly on His heart and mind. Let the name you write on your hand be a reminder to follow through on what you can do to show the love of Jesus to that person.

Solomon observed a very real contradiction in the lives of the foolish old man and the poor, wise young man. He reminds us fame is fleeting, but making a difference in the lives of others is eternal. I'd like to paraphrase Ecclesiastes 4:16: *"There are a sea of people out there cheering on the young new king, but that will fade and those who come after him won't even remember his name. It's empty . . . all the applause and adulation, it's gone in a moment, so live for eternity."*

Life doesn't always make sense, does it? But God has graciously given us His Word to help us deal with the oxymora of life. So, let's take a look at how we can live what we have learned out loud.

"Better is the poor who walks in his integrity Than one who is perverse in his lips, and is a fool."

Proverbs 19:1

1) Don't judge a book by its cover.
Name someone you may have been judging and pray the Lord will help you see them through the eyes of His love.

____

____

____

____

____

2) Persevere through adversity.
Are you allowing your difficult circumstances to *define* your character or *display* your character? Explain your answer.

____

____

____

____

____

____

3) Make this life count by making an eternal difference for others.
To whom are you ministering right now?

____

____

____

____

____

Are you motivated by Jesus to love them? ____________ Do you see that your actions can somehow point them to Jesus? Explain.

____

____

____

____

____

____

Let's go over this week's memory verse and finish the thought that follows.
"For My thoughts are not your thoughts, nor are your ways My ways, says the L*ORD. For as the heavens are higher than the earth, so are My ways higher than your ways, and My thoughts than your thoughts."* Isaiah 55:8, 9

Learning this verse has helped me ______________________________

____

____

____

____

____

____

____

____

____ .

Notes

4

The Serious Side of Life

It is healthy for us to laugh and have fun, but there are times when we need to take life seriously. This week we will study a variety of circumstances that God calls us to take seriously.

"For the grace of God that brings salvation has appeared to all men, teaching us that, denying ungodliness and worldly lusts, we should live soberly, righteously, and godly in this present age, looking for that blessed hope and glorious appearing of our great God and Savior Jesus Christ." Titus 2:11–13

DAY 1 Oh, Be Careful, Little Mouth, What You Say
DAY 2 Power, Position, and Possessions
DAY 3 Common among Men
DAY 4 Just Be Satisfied
DAY 5 Better Than . . .

Memory Verses

"Turn away my eyes from looking at worthless things, and revive me in Your way. Establish Your word to Your servant who is devoted to fearing You." Psalm 119:37–38

There are times when we need to take life seriously.

The Serious Side of Life

DAY ONE

OH, BE CAREFUL, LITTLE MOUTH, WHAT YOU SAY

Ecclesiastes 5:1–7

Life has changed significantly in the past hundred years, hasn't it? Lifestyles once considered immoral and offensive are now embraced and applauded. We see the world calling what is wrong right and what is right wrong. There seems to be an overall lack of respect for the things we once held dear and sacred: life, the young, the old, family, marriage, Christianity, church, and God.

Perhaps society has changed its standards, but God has not changed His. He is the same yesterday, today, and forever. He is holy and He calls us to live holy lives. We are to have a sense of awe and reverence for the One who created and sustains us. He holds our very lives in His hands and we must not allow our familiarity with the Lord to minimize our reverence for Him.

Today, we are going to study the subject of reverence. We will learn how we should approach God and why it is important to let our words be few.

Below, you will find Ecclesiastes 5:1–7 as it is translated in *The Message*, a paraphrase of the Bible. Please read it carefully, then answer the questions following it.

> 1. Watch your step when you enter God's house. Enter to learn. That's far better than mindlessly offering a sacrifice, doing more harm than good. Don't shoot off your mouth, or speak before you think. 2. Don't be too quick to tell God what you think he wants to hear. God's in charge, not you—the less you speak, the better. 3. Over-work makes for restless sleep. Over-talk shows you up as a fool. 4. When you tell God you'll do something, do it—now. God takes no pleasure in foolish gabble. Vow it, then do it. 5. Far better not to vow in the first place than to vow and not pay up. 6. Don't let your mouth make a total sinner of you. When called to account, you won't get by with "Sorry, I didn't mean it." Why risk provoking God to angry retaliation? 7. But against all illusion and fantasy and empty talk there's always this rock foundation: Fear God!

"In the multitude of words sin is not lacking, But he who restrains his lips is wise."

Proverbs 10:19

What is Solomon's first admonition in verse 1?

___

___

What do you think is the main theme of verses 2 through 6?

___

___

___

___

___

What seems to be the overriding decree in verse 7?

Did you notice how verse 1 begins with our need to approach God with reverence, and verse 7 ends with the same counsel? Clearly, Solomon is urging us to maintain an attitude of admiration, respect, and holy fear when we enter the presence of the Lord.

Much like Solomon, Moses also recognized our need to approach God with reverential fear. In Exodus 3, Moses had a close encounter of the Divine kind when he spotted a burning bush in the distance. As he began to draw closer to it, the Lord spoke to him: *"Do not come near; put your shoes off your feet, for the place on which you stand is holy ground"* (Exodus 3:5 AMP). Now, if you travel to Exodus 33:9–11 with me, you will see that the LORD spoke with Moses as a man speaks with a friend. But Moses' accessibility to the Lord did not diminish his reverence for Him.

I remember that when I was young, my mom would holler at us after she finished vacuuming, "You'd better make sure you take your shoes off before you come in the house!" We didn't really understand what the big deal was, but we obeyed her because we respected her. We were also sure that if we didn't do what she said we'd end up wishing we had.

". . . he heard the voice of One speaking to him from above the mercy seat . . ."

Numbers 7:89

The burning bush was a place where God revealed Himself to Moses in a new and profound way. It was the place where God called Moses to do the impossible. But it was also a place of reverence where a holy God met with an imperfect man. The flames from the burning bush may have kindled Moses' curiosity, but permission to approach the presence of the Living God and step across the threshold of the natural and enter into the presence of the Divine would only be granted when Moses took off his shoes.

📖 Now let's look at Exodus 34:6–9 and answer the following questions. How did Moses respond to God (verse 8)?

In verse 9 we see Moses' prayer to the Lord. What attitude does Moses display?

God may have chosen to speak to Moses as a friend but He did not cease to be God. God is God . . . He is the Great I AM, He is Elohim, He is the Alpha and Omega, He is the Righteous One, He is the Holy One, He is THE Lord! He has no beginning; He has no end; He has no limitations; He has no equal. He, alone, is the Lord! We are constrained to revere God by the sheer essence of His being.

Please read John 15:14, 15. What does Jesus call His disciples?

____

Yes, the Lord has called us friends, but we are not His equal. Our friendship with the Lord is a precious relationship Christ has secured for those who trust in Him, but, like Moses, we need to understand that our friendship with Him in no way minimizes His holiness. Our attitude before Him should always be one of humility, worship, and reverential fear.

Our attitude before Him should always be one of humility, worship, and reverential fear.

Now let's turn back to Ecclesiastes 5:1. The second part of that verse shows us two very opposite ends of the spectrum. On the one end, we have the right way to approach God: with a ready ear and a willing heart. On the other end, we see the wrong way to approach God: with a hasty heart and a foolish sacrifice.

This verse seems to shout Cain and Abel to me. In Genesis 4:2–5 we find that both these boys brought sacrifices to the Lord. Abel brought a sacrifice of the firstborn of his flock and Cain brought an offering of the fruit of the ground. Literally, a fruit of his own labor. The Bible is basically silent as to how Abel knew that God required an animal sacrifice but it speaks very loudly to the fact Abel was well aware of what type of sacrifice the Lord would accept. That means that at one time or another, Abel, with a willing and obedient heart, listened to his parents or to the Lord Himself tell him what type of sacrifice God demanded. Cain, on the other hand, may have known what was required, but he chose to bring a sacrifice of fools and offer the work of his own hands.

How unfortunate that Cain didn't even realize what he did was evil. What a good example of what Ecclesiastes 5:1 means when it says, ". . . rather than give the sacrifice of fools, for they do not know that they do evil."

There are many ways in which we can offer a sacrifice of fools, but they all begin with a lack of readiness to hear from and obey the Lord. A fool thinks he can impress God with his great sacrifices, long prayers, and zealous vows, but God is not fooled by these "religious" acts, because He sees the individual's heart. A fool thinks he can dismiss God and ignore His instructions without consequence.

Let's look at what type of attitude we should have to enter into the presence of the Lord.

Please read the following passages of Scripture and fill in the blanks.
1 Samuel 3:9, 10: *"Go lie down; and it shall be, if He calls you, that you must say, '________, Lord, for Your servant __________.'" Now the Lord came and stood and called as at other times, "Samuel! Samuel!" And Samuel answered, "__________, for Your servant __________."*

At this point, I'd like for you to reflect on your own worship experience with the Lord. Do you enter His presence telling Him all your needs and woes without giving Him time to truly speak to your heart? Or, like Samuel, do you say, *"I'm listening, What do you want me to do?"*? (Contemporary English Version)

Now look again at Ecclesiastes 5:2–6 and fill in the blanks.

Verse 2: *"Do not be rash with your* ____________________*."*
Verse 2: *"Let your* ____________ *be few."*
Verse 3: *"A fool's voice is known by his many* ____________________*."*
Verse 4: *"When you make a* ________ *to God, do not delay to pay it."*
Verse 5: *"Better not to* ____________________ *than to* ______________ *and not pay."*
Verse 6: *"Do not let your* ____________ *cause your flesh to sin."*

These verses remind us God is interested in what comes out of our mouths. There's a cute little song we still sing in Sunday School classes that goes like this: "Oh, be careful, little mouth, what you say; Oh, be careful, little mouth, what you say, for the Father up above is looking down with love, so be careful, little mouth, what you say." I believe this song must have originated in the heart of someone who understood the significance of Ecclesiastes 5:2.

We will conclude today's lesson by looking at two aspects of what God's Word tells us about what we say. First, we'll look at the need to let our words be few. Then, we'll take a look at the biblical principle of making vows.

Ecclesiastes 5:2 teaches us to guard what comes out of our mouths. In fact, God's Word speaks extensively about what we do and do not say. Let's begin with a little guided tour of some clear verses on the subject.

📖 Please look up each verse and fill in the blank.
James 1:19: *". . . let every man be swift to* ____________*, slow to* __________ ____________*."*

Proverbs 10:19: *"In the multitude of* __________ __________ *is not lacking, but he who restrains his* _______ *is* ________*."*

Proverbs 10:31, 32: *"The mouth of the righteous brings forth* ___________*, but the perverse* ___________ *will be cut out. The* ________ *of the righteous know what is* ________________ *but the* ____________ *of the wicked is* ____________*."*

Proverbs 15:2: *"The tongue of the* ________ *uses knowledge rightly, but the* __________ *of fools* ________________ *foolishness."*

A wise woman thinks before she speaks.

Proverbs 29:11: *"A fool* ___________ *all his feelings, but a wise man* ___________ *back."*

The main lesson found in each of these verses is that a wise woman will guard what she says. She thinks before she speaks. She has a keen awareness God is in heaven and that she will give an account to Him one day for *"every idle word"* (Matthew 12:36). The fool, on the other hand, lives her life under the sun without regard to her day of reckoning . . . therefore, she isn't really concerned about what she says or does not say. Like a broken fire hydrant, she just spews whatever comes to her mind.

In Ecclesiastes 5:3, we find an interesting comparison. Constant dreaming is a sign our lives are excessively busy, and one who finds herself constantly running off at the mouth gives evidence that she is a foolish woman, not understanding the importance of letting her words be few.

Although Solomon has been cautioning us about what we say, he becomes more specific in verse 4 and begins discussing the subject of vows. A vow is a voluntary pledge to fulfill an agreement and when used in the Bible, it's almost always used in reference to a vow to God. Solomon uses the next three verses to remind us of the seriousness of making a vow.

📖 Please read the following verses and fill in the blanks.
Deuteronomy 23:21–23: *"When you make a _______ to the Lord your God, you shall not delay to ______ it; for the Lord your God will surely _________ it of you, and it would be __________ to you. But if you abstain from __________, it shall not be ____________ to you. That which has gone from your ____________ you shall _________ and ___________, for you __________ vowed to the Lord your God what you have __________ with your _______________."*

In these verses we find that a vow must be voluntary and once made, it is binding. It's kind of like the old hymn, "No turning back, no turning back."

"That which has gone from your lips you shall keep and perform . . ."
Deuteronomy 23:23

Have you ever heard of the term "sickbed vows"? That's a promise people make to the Lord while they're sick, but as soon as they're well, they conveniently forget what they promised to the Lord. They may forget, but God certainly doesn't. He requires the fulfillment of each vow we make. Numbers 30:2 and Proverbs 20:25 give us the same warning. Likewise, Ecclesiastes 5:6 reminds us that once we have made a vow to the Lord, it's foolish to try to say, "Oops! I really didn't mean it!" Now, that would be a good example of a sacrifice of fools.

Today, the value of wedding vows is at an all-time low. The divorce rate in the church is just as high as it is in the world. Many people just don't seem to take their wedding vows seriously. "For better or for worse" and " 'Til death do us part" often don't really mean what they say.

Now hang on, girls, because we're getting ready to discuss some touchy subjects, and I want to warn you, this may get personal. We tend to think we're keeping our wedding vows simply because we are hanging in there, refusing to allow the "D" word to ever become an option. But on the day you said, "I do," I'm sure your vows included a lot more than just "'Til death do us part." I know mine sure did.

For most of us, we made vows that include words such as *love, honor, cherish, putting his needs before our own, for richer or for poorer, in sickness and in health.* You see, our vows extend way beyond the decision to "just stay together." Some of our vows even included the dreaded word *obey*. What? . . . *obey*! Did any of us actually say that? Do we really have to obey? Well, let's go back to God's Word. Look at Ecclesiastes 5:6 in *The Message*: *"Don't let your mouth make a total sinner of you. When called to account, you won't get by with "Sorry, I didn't mean it." Why risk provoking God to angry retaliation?"*

If you said it, you are accountable to keep it. I know that's not popular now, but God's Word is God's Word . . . and our accountability to God does not change because we live in a different place and time. A vow is a vow and we can't go running to God picking and choosing the parts of the marriage vows we want to keep. The Bible says that when we do that, we make a total sinner out of ourselves and provoke God.

We need to take ALL our vows very seriously. And for those who are contemplating marriage, think about the vows you're going to make and be sure you're willing to fulfill that to which you commit before God. It's serious business.

As we review today's lesson, we see we have primarily covered two very important topics: our reverence for God and the need to carefully guard our lips. Solomon concludes his thoughts on the matter by saying, "Fear God" (v. 7). The Bible tells us the fear of the Lord is the beginning of wisdom. Our reverential fear of God will prompt us to live as we ought in our journey under the sun.

So as we close today's lesson, I want to encourage you to let your words be few. That's obviously easier said than done—but it is doable. God's Word sweetly reminds us ALL things are possible with God and that we can do ALL things through Christ who strengthens us—even the most talkative of us. Yes . . . God is a God of miracles, isn't He?!

Don't forget to study your memory verses today!
"Turn away my eyes from looking at worthless things, and revive me in Your way. Establish Your word to Your servant who is devoted to fearing You." Psalm 119:37, 38

LIFE APPLICATION TIP
If you're married, review your wedding vows and ask the Lord to help you place the same level of importance on them as He calls you to. Also, take the time to evaluate the words you say and the promises you have made. Ask the Lord to help you be more aware of your accountability before Him for every idle word.

The Serious Side of Life

DAY TWO

POWER AND POSSESSIONS

We don't get another chance to do this thing called life.

Ecclesiastes 5:8–20

As I sit here praying over you and seeking God's face to discern the words He wants me to use to convey Ecclesiastes 5:8–20, my mind keeps shifting to the prevailing motivation I have for reading, studying, and teaching God's Word. That motivation is that I may know Him more, that I may make Him and His Word known, and that His Word will make a difference in me and you—not just an insignificant superficial difference, but a life-altering, Jesus-honoring, being-the-real-deal difference.

We don't get another chance to do this thing called *life*. This is not a dress rehearsal for the real thing—this *is* the real thing. The wisdom needed to make this life count for more than a vapor beckons us to listen intently to Solomon's words of wisdom—even when it hurts. If we choose to turn a deaf ear we may just find ourselves chasing the wind like the rest of the world.

True love, power, possessions, and prominence: four of life's most elusive (and illusory) desires. In today's lesson, Solomon brings us face-to-face with two potentially promising, often debilitating, pursuits: the pursuit of power and the pursuit of possessions.

📖 Take a few minutes and read Ecclesiastes 5:8, 9 in as many Bible versions as you can. See if you can decipher these two verses, and write your conclusions here:

____

____

____

____

____

____

____

"Power tends to corrupt, and absolute power corrupts absolutely."

Lord Acton once said, "Power tends to corrupt, and absolute power corrupts absolutely. Great men are almost always bad men." It's an unfortunate reality that corruption frequently accompanies power. Perhaps every form of government known to man is intrinsically linked to some sort of corruption, but Ecclesiastes 5:8, 9 reminds us that a twisted government is generally better than no government at all.

Unfortunately, power is both intoxicating and addictive. Those in authority sometimes abuse their power because they lose sight of reality. Their own perception of themselves is frequently distorted and they begin to think more highly of themselves than they ought. Maybe that's why Solomon said, *"Don't be too surprised when you see the poor kicked around and justice and right violated all over the place"* (v. 8, MSG).

Remember, at some point in time Solomon checked out on God. He put God on a shelf and decided to make this life all about himself. He wanted to do this life under the sun on his own terms. After years of wandering in his own direction, however, he realized it was all vanity, and Ecclesiastes became his exposition on what really matters most. Isn't it funny that the human race hasn't really changed at all?

Solomon takes us from power in verses 8 and 9 to possessions in verses 10 through 17. He begins to sing a familiar tune as he once again reminds us there is no satisfaction to be found in the accumulation and abundance of possessions or personal wealth. Instead, there is often a plethora of problems that come with being wealthy. So before you go wishing you were on the Forbes Annual Billionaires List, let's look at a few of the troubles the affluent often face.

1) Wealth often brings feelings of emptiness because it cannot satisfy. We are inundated with the concept that if we just had masses of money, we'd all be happy. Ecclesiastes 5:10 makes a case for just the opposite. In fact, no matter how much money we acquire, as the song says, we still "can't get no satisfaction." Think about it. When was the last time that something you had bought brought you happiness for more than a week or two?

Below is 1 Timothy 6:6–10. Compare it with your Bible and then fill in the blanks.

"Now godliness with _______________ is great ___________. For we brought _______________ into this world, and it is certain we can carry _______________ out. And having _______________ and _______________, with

these we shall be content. But those who ___________ to be rich fall into _________________ and a snare, and into many _____________ and __________ lusts which _____________ men in __________ and ________________. For the ___________ of money is the root of _______________ of evil, for which some have _______________ from the ___________ in their ___________, and _______________ themselves through with many ______________."

That passage seems to be a commentary on Ecclesiastes 5:10–17, doesn't it? These verses remind us that if we think money can buy happiness, we're fooling ourselves.

If we think money can buy happiness, we're fooling ourselves.

2) Wealth frequently causes a lack of trust in personal relationships. Ecclesiastes 5:11 in the New Living Translation tells us, *"The more you have, the more people come to help you spend it. So what good is wealth—except perhaps to watch it slip through your fingers!"*

I've known a few wealthy people in my time, and I've watched countless interviews with the rich and famous, and they all say the same thing: "We don't know who we can trust." Before they hit the big time, they were just average Joes who had real friends they went bowling with or to a ball game. They were friends they could actually count on. When they became wealthy, people started coming out of the woodwork pretending to be their friends in order to get a handout. Excess money leads to friendships that are almost always questionable.

Solomon echoes that same truth in Proverbs 14:20: *"The poor man is hated even by his own neighbor, but the rich has many friends."* Proverbs 19:4 tells us, *"Wealth makes many friends, but the poor is separated from his neighbor."*

3) Wealth generally brings anxiety. Notice in Ecclesiastes 5:12, the wealthy man loses sleep while the laborer's sleep is sweet.

Why do you think that is true?

____

____

____

____

____

The more possessions we have, the more our possessions have us . . . our time and our efforts. Wealth keeps our mind racing on how to keep what we have, and then how to make more. So we lose sleep worrying about the next business deal, or how we can get the next big thing. Wealth doesn't bring peace; on the contrary, it frequently brings pressure.

4) Wealth is fleeting. Ecclesiastes 5:13–17 tells us of the elusive nature of money. It's like sand through our fingers. No matter how hard we try to hold on to it, it has the propensity to escape our grasp. The stark reality is, whether we are rich or poor . . . one event happens to us all. Remember, death is the great equalizer and no matter how much we gain, we can't take anything with us when we go.

So, what are we to do? How are we to live this life God has given us under the sun? In Ecclesiastes 5:18–20, Solomon turns his (and our) attention toward God, and reminds us of what truly brings joy and contentment in this life. In the Hebrew, verse 18 actually says, *"Behold, I have seen what is beautiful . . ."* In other words, it's a beautiful thing to find contentment with the lot in life that God has given us. Does that mean we aren't to try to do better for ourselves? Does it mean we're not to buy things or save any money? Of course not!

First Timothy 6:17–19 says,

> *"Command those who are rich in this present age not to be haughty, nor to trust in uncertain riches but in the living God, who gives us richly all things to enjoy. Let them do good, that they be rich in good works, ready to give, willing to share, storing up for themselves a good foundation for the time to come, that they may lay hold on eternal life."*

We looked at this verse when we studied Ecclesiastes 2, but the frequency with which Scripture instructs us about how we view our finances reveals our need for constant reminders. Kind of like nonstop Post-it notes all through the Bible. This world cries out to us to get more . . . to get as much as we can . . . to be rich . . . to be famous. Solomon cries out to us to understand that everything we have is a gift from God . . . to put our trust in God, not in our wealth . . . to understand that life is short and eternity is long. So you can see why intentionally living life for eternity is not only a biblical mandate, but it also just makes sense to live our few years here on Earth with our focus on that which will never end.

". . . [the tranquillity of God is mirrored in him]."

We conclude today's lesson with Ecclesiastes 5:20, and I love the way it reads in the Amplified Bible: *"For he shall not much remember [seriously] the days of his life, because God [Himself] answers and corresponds to the joy of his heart [the tranquillity of God is mirrored in him]."* Even the difficult days lose their sting, and time seems to heal all wounds when God speaks peace and joy into our lives. When our hearts are set on seeking God rather than pursuing power and possessions, God's tranquility, His peace, is mirrored in our lives. That means we have the capacity to reflect God's peace and it becomes obvious to others that we are resting in the Lord, even when this world has gone mad.

When I started today's lesson, I reflected on my motivation for reading, studying, and teaching God's Word. It is so I may know Him, that I may make Him and His Word known, and that His Word will make a real difference in my life and the lives of those I have the privilege to teach. Today, I am reminded we serve a loving God, who has given us clear instruction on how to live this life, under the sun, and how to truly make it count for more than a vapor. His Word reminds me the pursuit of power and possessions is like chasing the wind. It will leave me empty. It will leave you empty, too.

Today, I know Him more. I know that even though I'm not powerful or wealthy, He loves me and has my best interests at heart. Today, I'm reminded neither power nor possessions have the capacity to define me. I understand that God has a plan for my life. He alone gives me peace and contentment, and knowing this truth makes me want to live this life, under the sun, as a big "Thank You" card to God for all He has given me.

I pray that you will live for the Lord in such a way that God's peace and joy will be mirrored in your life. I also pray that you will see the fruitlessness of pursuing power or possessions. God gives us all things to enjoy, so smile, my friend, and remember . . . life is short, eternity is long . . . so live for eternity.

Don't forget to study this week's memory verses.
"Turn away my eyes from looking at worthless things, and revive me in Your way. Establish Your word to Your servant who is devoted to fearing You." Psalm 119:37, 38

LIFE APPLICATION TIP
Make a list of things that catch your eye and have a tendency to distract you from pursuing that which is eternal. Ask the Lord to help you put those distractions aside for the beauty of knowing Him more.

The Serious Side of Life

DAY THREE

COMMON AMONG MEN

Ecclesiastes 6:1–8

Have you ever noticed that when you go to a baby shower the women there tend to talk about their own birthing experiences? We do that because it's something we're familiar with, and with which we can relate to the shower-ee. It's very common for people to talk about subjects they are familiar with, and Solomon was no different. So while it may seem as though he's singing the same old song, today we're going to look at some different lyrics to the same old tune while we survey Solomon's final attempt to convey the vanity of riches to us.

Because of his own personal position and wealth, Solomon was well-acquainted with the snares that often accompany an abundant supply of power and possessions. He wasn't just *talking about* the lifestyles of the rich and famous, he was *living* the life of the rich and famous. Let's just say he had an insider's view and he wanted us to see things from his perspective.

"Riches do not profit in the day of wrath, But righteousness delivers from death."

Proverbs 11:4

To get an insight into Solomon's perspective on the subject of riches, let's look at the following verses and some questions they raise.

📖 Please read Ecclesiastes 3:13.
What is the gift of God?

____

____

____

📖 Turn to Ecclesiastes 5:18, 19.
According to verse 18, what is good and fitting?

____

____

____

According to verse 19, God gives riches, wealth and the __________ to eat of it to receive his heritage and rejoice in his labor—this is the __________ of God.

📖 Next read Ecclesiastes 6:1, 2.

According to these verses, there is a common occurrence among mankind, and that is, *"God has given riches and __________________ and ____________, so that his soul lacks __________________ of all that he __________; yet God has not ______________ him to eat from them, but a foreigner ________________ them. This is vanity and a severe __________."*

Now let's do a little comparison so we can really get a better picture of what Solomon is teaching us about riches.

Ecclesiastes 5:18, 19	Ecclesiastes 6:1, 2
• Solomon sees what is good and fitting.	• Solomon sees an evil among men.
• God gives man riches and wealth.	• God gives man riches, wealth, and honor.
• God gives man power to enjoy His gifts.	• God doesn't give power to enjoy His gifts.
• This is the gift of God.	• This is vanity and a severe affliction.

"... This night your soul will be required of you; then whose will those things be ..."

Luke 12:20

We are actually looking at two sides of the same coin, the coin of wealth given to mankind by God. However, in contrast, even though the Ecclesiastes 5 man squandered and poorly invested his money, at least he got to enjoy what the Lord had bestowed upon him. The Ecclesiastes 6 man is not given the power or the capacity to enjoy what he has been given.

Solomon readily acknowledged the Giver of the gifts, but as he looked around, he saw something the Contemporary English Version calls *"terribly unfair"* and the New Living Translation calls a *"serious tragedy"*—the inability many have to enjoy the financial and material blessings God has given them. He doesn't go into detail why so many who are wealthy lack the capacity to enjoy what they have. He just describes it as a prevalent occurrence.

As we look at the lifestyles of the rich and famous today, we see that things aren't really any different from when Solomon reigned as the richest man in the world. In fact, if you turn your television on and watch a few clips of celebrity news, you'll find that although they have more money and fame than they know what to do with, they lack the capacity to enjoy their status. For them, there is no such thing as hanging out with the girls at Starbucks; it's impossible to just spend the day strolling through the mall or the outlet shops. Hounded by the flashbulbs of the paparazzi leaves them little time to truly revel in their riches.

I recently read an article by Jonathan Clements in the *Wall Street Journal Online* entitled, "Rich, Successful—and Miserable: New Research Probes Mid-Life Angst." Here's his opening paragraph: "If you're in your 40s, you are probably pulling down a bigger paycheck than ever before, and your portfolio has never been fatter. And yet, if research by economists and psychologists is any guide, you've never been more miserable."[5]

We may not know why, but it is really very common for those who are extremely wealthy to experience little happiness. Sometimes, it's unexpected health issues that prevent the wealthy from enjoying their blessings; maybe it's due to a family crisis or an unhappy home life, or possibly, one bad decision after another; perhaps it's the loneliness that often accompanies wealth because it creates a lack of trust; maybe it's the need for greed that keeps them on the edge, always looking for a way to make a buck and always worrying about losing what they have. How unfortunate! That which they work so hard to obtain becomes the source of discontentment and unhappiness. Sometimes, it even becomes the cause of their failing health. A. J. Reb Materi once said, "So many people spend their health gaining wealth, and then have to spend their wealth to regain their health."[6]

Oftentimes, those who are wealthy find themselves in a quest for the elusive luxury of enjoying their gain and end up, as Jonathan Clements so aptly put it, "miserable." That's true for those whose "quest" is fame or fortune; for those who have become enamored with the lifestyles of the rich and famous; for those who make material possessions their passion.

In a world where we are prone to be "material girls," Ecclesiastes gives us a very basic biblical principle that can help us overcome this "miserable" condition. It is that our motivation is to be rooted in our passion to know the Lord, not our passion to have stuff or our passion to make this life be all about us.

As Solomon viewed the world "under the sun," he was well aware of the constant appeal of riches, but he was also personally acquainted with the emptiness that often accompanies wealth. In Ecclesiastes 5:10, Solomon writes, *"He who loves money will not be satisfied with money, nor he who loves abundance with its income. This too is vanity."* Psalm 115:4 tells us that the idols of those who don't know the Lord are silver and gold.

Instead of seeking to be rich, we are to *". . . keep seeking those things that are above, where Christ is seated on the right hand of God. Set [our] minds on things above, not on things of the earth"* (Colossians 3:1, 2). The motivation of our hearts is to be our passion to know the Lord and to make Him known. When our focus becomes the acquiring of wealth and material possessions, then we're not only missing the point to our purpose, but we're also engaging in self-idolatry. Idolatry is glorification, adulation, or placing an abundance of our attention on anything other than God. It is setting our affections on things of the earth instead of the God who created this earth. The distractions of life can cause us to get so wrapped up in the gift that we forget to give glory to the Giver.

"Set your minds on things above, not on things of the earth."

Colossians 3:2

You can lack nothing this life has to offer, you can have everything you desire, but if you don't have the capacity to enjoy any of it, it is vanity . . . empty . . . futile . . . worthless.

As we continue in today's lesson, we are brought to a very harsh reality in Ecclesiastes 6:3: A man can live an entire lifetime and never garner the love and respect of family and friends. During Solomon's day, it was very important for the children to honor their parents with a good burial. Yet, Solomon described a man who had not lived well enough to gain the respect and honor necessary to merit a decent funeral. Solomon said it would have been better for him to never have been born than to live a lonely, miserable, and pitiful life.

At the beginning of today's lesson, we did a little comparison. I'd like for us to do another one that will help us understand how we can avoid the same unfortunate fate as those we studied in verses 1 through 3 of Ecclesiastes 6. On the flip side, it will help us understand what matters most as we learn to live a full and meaningful life, under the sun.

What Can Satisfy?

📖 Please read Psalm 36:7, 8. Who are satisfied, and with what?

____

____

📖 Next read Psalm 107:8, 9. Who satisfies the longing soul?

____

____

____

📖 Also please read Psalm 145:16. Who satisfies the desire of every living thing?

____

____

"You open Your hand And satisfy the desire of every living thing."
Psalm 145:16

📖 Read Jeremiah 31:14. What satisfies God's people?

____

____

What Cannot Satisfy?

📖 Turn to Proverbs 27:24. How long will riches last?

____

____

____

📖 Please read Ecclesiastes 1:8. What two things are not able to satisfy?

____

____

📖 Read next Ezekiel 7:19. What won't satisfy and what became their stumbling block?

____

____

📖 Read Revelation 3:14–19. What was the Lord's rebuke to the Laodicean church?

____

____

____

____

We can have all the things money can buy and still be miserable, poor, and blind. A heart preoccupied with acquiring more stuff casts a colossal shadow on that which money is incapable of buying: things like love, friendships, respect, honor, loyalty, godliness, a good reputation, trustworthiness, dependability, and humility. Those who pursue the external riches of this world tend to skip over the internal riches of a God-centered and God-honoring life. They fall prey to the lures of this world and all it offers. Their focus is set on obtaining wealth, fame, and success, and their vision is so narrow they don't even realize they haven't been given the capacity to enjoy what they have. Their wealth becomes a subtle distraction from their personal relationship with God and they forsake His fellowship for the pursuit of prosperity.

Ecclesiastes 6:4–8 continues to give us the lowdown on the outcome of a life lived in pursuit of prosperity. Solomon tries to warn us of the detours riches often cause us to take in this journey called *life.* He understood that our pursuit of knowing and pleasing God must supersede all other pursuits; he realized the only way any of us can experience true joy, true peace, and true satisfaction is to seek the Lord above all other aspirations.

Matthew 6:33 tells us we are to seek first the kingdom of God and His righteousness and all these things will be added to us. What things? Those things found in the context of Matthew 6:19–34. So, let's conclude today's lesson by looking at those verses and answering the following questions.

Verse 19: What are we not to do, and why not?

____

____

____

Verse 20: What are we told to do?

____

____

____

Verse 21: What does your "storage bin" say about your heart?

____

____

____

Verse 24: Why is it impossible to serve God *and* wealth?

____

____

____

Verse 25: What are we not to worry about?

____

____

____

"Do not love the world or the things in the world . . ."

I John 2:15

Verses 26–30: List the examples used to demonstrate the way God provides for His creation.

Verse 33: What is to be the priority of our pursuits and what will be the end result if we keep our priorities in order?

APPLY Now, let's get personal. Do you struggle with being materialistically motivated?

What do you find yourself pursuing?

Have you jeopardized any relationship for the sake of empty pursuits? If so, please share your experience here.

"But seek ye first the kingdom of God and His righteousness . . ." Matthew 6:33

Solomon has given us some food for thought in Ecclesiastes 6:1–8. We find ourselves having to evaluate our own lives in light of Scripture. Understanding what matters most means understanding what matters most to the Lord. He makes it very clear we are to seek . . . pursue . . . be zealous for the kingdom of God and His righteousness *first*. When we do that, He will see to it that, like the birds of the air, we will not only have our needs taken care of, we'll also delight in the breathtaking view as we fly with wings of eagles, making the Lord the relentless pursuit of our lives.

Enjoy the abundant life that comes from knowing Him, by seeking to live a holy and righteous life, and by encouraging others to do the same. That's what living a "rich" life is all about. I am very sure that when we live that rich life, we will garner the love and respect from others that the Ecclesiastes 6:3 man was incapable of getting.

MEMORY VERSE

"Turn away my eyes from looking at worthless things, and revive me in Your way. Establish Your word to Your servant who is devoted to fearing You." Psalm 119:37, 38

MEMORY TIP
Take your verses with you when you go walking, and practice them over and over again.

The Serious Side of Life

DAY FOUR

JUST BE CONTENT

Ecclesiastes 6:7–12

Here we are a little past midway through our study of Ecclesiastes, and I'm so thankful you have taken this journey with me. I may not know your name, but you have been the object of many of my prayers. I desperately desire that when we come to the end of this study, we will have an unshakable perspective of what really matters most in this life we all live, under the sun.

Yesterday, we took a look at Solomon's final treatise on the various pitfalls of riches. Today, we will have the opportunity to look at the failure to find satisfaction in the labor of our hands and the need to be content where we are . . . in our little lot in life.

Begin by reading the Amplified Bible version of Ecclesiastes 6:7, 8:

> *"All the labor of man is for his mouth [for self-preservation and enjoyment], and yet his desire is not satisfied. For what advantage has the wise man over the fool [being worldly-wise is not the secret to happiness]? What advantage has the poor man who has learned how to walk before the living [publicly, with men's eyes upon him; being poor is not the secret to happiness either]?"*

"Now godliness with contentment is great gain."
I Timothy 6:6

Solomon gives us another glance at our responsibility to work in order to provide for our basic needs and for the things we enjoy doing. The mandate to work is actually one of the results of the curse (Genesis 3:17–19). He uses an example to remind us that no matter how hard we work, no matter how much we acquire—even by the sweat of our brow—we are never completely satisfied. Just as it doesn't take long for our bellies to growl after we've eaten a meal, it doesn't take long for the desires of our flesh and our hearts to growl for more, either. Verse 8 continues to remind us that whether rich or poor, wise or a fool, there is no advantage, because we all have insatiable appetites for more.

📖 Please read 1 Thessalonians 4:11, 12 and fill in the blanks.
". . . and to make it your ________________ *to lead a quiet life and* ________ *to your own* ____________________ *and* ____________ *with your* __________, *just as we commanded you, so that you will behave properly toward outsiders and not be in any* ______________________*."*

As Christians, our work ethic is a very important part of our testimony. It's our chance to shine from 9 to 5. In a world filled with darkness and confusion, we have an opportunity to bring light and clarity to those around us for the glory of the Lord.

First Corinthians 10:31 reminds us that even if we are eating or drinking—in fact, whatever we do—we are to do it for God's glory. Colossians 3:23 instructs us to work "heartily" as for the Lord rather than for men.

That means whether I'm cleaning toilets, washing clothes, teaching children, selling advertising, or running a major corporation, I'm to do it as if I'm doing it for the Lord and with the goal of glorifying the Lord. The Bible tells us in John 6:27 we are not to labor for food that perishes, but for that which will endure forever.

APPLY So let's get personal for a minute. When's the last time you actually cleaned a toilet "heartily"?

____

____

____

Does your boss see you put forth your very best effort? ____________

Our lives should reflect who we are, whether we are at home, at work, at the grocery store, or running other errands—laboring for the eternal, not the temporal.

As we move forward in our study of Ecclesiastes 6, let's take a look at verses 9 and 10 in the Amplified Bible: *"Better is the sight of the eyes [the enjoyment of what is available to one] than the cravings of wandering desire. This is also vanity (emptiness, falsity, and futility) and a striving after the wind and a feeding on it! Whatever [man] is, he has been named that long ago, and it is known that it is man [Adam]; nor can he contend with Him who is mightier than he [whether God or death]."*

We've all seen people spend their lives chasing an elusive dream.

What a vivid account of chasing after the wind of unattainable (and frequently unhealthy) desires! We've all known someone who has left a spouse to chase after someone who wasn't half the person their spouse was. We've all seen people spend their lives chasing an elusive dream. They just can't enjoy where they are in their pursuit of where they want to be. They forsake the pleasure of today in search of the pot of gold at the end of the rainbow. Have you ever known anyone who really found the pot of gold? Neither have I!

Solomon wanted us to see there is a huge blessing associated with understanding, accepting, and enjoying our lot in life. He isn't telling us we shouldn't dream or that we shouldn't be ambitious. But he is telling us we shouldn't waste our time chasing after empty dreams. The Lord is to be the pursuit of our lives, and when He becomes the One we seek to know and please, He establishes and brings to pass everything we need in order to live a full and meaningful life. He enables us to find fulfillment in this life we all live, under the sun. He, alone, can satisfy the longing of our souls.

When we hear the word *contentment* we generally think of needing to be content in our finances, our positions, and our relationships, but our need to be content is just as real in our spiritual lives. It is a biblical principle that calls us to find a very peculiar balance, because it requires we find our contentment in the Lord—while ambitiously serving Him. With that in mind it is important we understand that *contentment* does not mean "lack of ambition or action."

I have often struggled with the biblical concept of contentment in the area of serving the Lord because I tend to *envision big!* You see, we serve the Creator of the universe and I am very confident He is able to do anything and everything He chooses. There is nothing too difficult for Him and the Bible teaches us that through Him, we can do all things. He actually specializes in taking the base and lowly of this world and using them to accomplish great things. If you're not sure about that, ask Peter what he did before the Lord told him, "Follow Me." Peter was a fisherman. Then there's Joseph . . . the youngest of the family, despised by his brothers and sold into slavery. He later obtained a position in Egypt second only to Pharaoh. What about Moses? He was just a baby in a basket whom God later used to deliver His people. And let's not forget about Rahab the harlot, or Mary—an unknown Jewish girl who became the mother of Jesus.

William Carey once said, "Attempt great things for God, expect great things from God." And so I envision big. However, it's important to keep in mind that while we may attempt great things for God, we must live where we are. In other words, we must learn to be content *and* faithful with each step of the journey.

We must learn to be content and faithful with each step of the journey.

Solomon's admonition is to "accept your lot in life" and to "play the hand you're dealt." "Be content" is a biblical call to rest in the sovereignty of God. As we clarify our understanding of and our need to be content, let's look at a few verses that give us a biblical perspective of contentment.

> Hebrews 13:5: *"Let your character or moral disposition be free from love of money [including greed, avarice, lust, and craving for earthly possessions] and be satisfied with your present [circumstances and with what you have]; for He [God] Himself has said, I will not in any way fail you nor give you up nor leave you without support. [I will] not,[I will] not, [I will] not in any degree leave you helpless nor forsake nor let [you] down (relax My hold on you)! [Assuredly not!]"* (AMP)

What is to be free from the love of money?

____

____

____

What are we to be content with?

____

____

____

What is the basis for our contentment?

____

____

____

You see, it is the presence of the Living God that not only *calls* me to be content, but also *enables* me to be content, because He is the Sovereign Lord over everything. I can rest in my present circumstances because I can rest in Him. I know He loves me and that He has a perfect and good plan for my life (Jeremiah 29:11); He has promised to complete that which He began in me (Philippians 1:6); and His abiding presence is the basis for my contentment (Hebrews 13:5).

Philippians 4:11–13 (NASB): *"Not that I speak from want, for I have learned to be content in whatever circumstances I am. I know how to get along with humble means, and I also know how to live in prosperity; in any and every circumstance I have learned the secret of being filled and going hungry, both of having abundance and suffering need. I can do all things through Him who strengthens me."*

What did Paul learn?

____

____

____

Who was the source of Paul's strength?

____

____

It is important to note that experience was Paul's teacher. The *How to Be Content* book can never teach us as much or as well as can life itself. Paul *learned* how to be content no matter what he was going through. Good or bad, Paul was content because he had learned to be content.

APPLY Now let's get personal . . . again. Are you content with your lot in life?__________

What (or who) is the source of your strength?

____

____

____

____

"... shall the thing formed say of him who formed it, 'He has no understanding'?"

Isaiah 29:16

Jeremiah 18:6 (NASB): *"Behold, like the clay in the potter's hand, so are you in My hand."*

Romans 9:20, 21 (NASB): *"On the contrary, who are you, O man, who answers back to God? The thing molded will not say to the molder, 'Why did you make me like this,' will it? Or does not the potter have a right over the clay, to make from the same lump one vessel for honorable use and another for common use?"*

According to these verses, who is the Potter and who is the clay?

____

____

____

What do you think Romans 9:20, 21 is saying?

____

____

____

____

God is God and He is in control. He is sovereign. We are to be moldable clay in the Potter's hand and we are to be content with how He chooses to fashion us. Our struggle to be content can be traced to our desire to pursue something other than the Lord, but contentment can only be found in making Christ the all-consuming passion and pursuit of our lives. He alone can bring contentment to a restless heart.

So, as we conclude our lesson today, I'd like to paraphrase Ecclesiastes 6:11, 12: *"The more words we use the more empty our words become. There are so many things that vie for our attention and our affection . . . and since our lives are like a shadow and no one really knows what is going to happen after he dies . . . just be content with your lot in life and live this life to the fullest."*

That sounds like good advice for all of us, doesn't it?!

APPLY Please take the time to finish today's lesson by evaluating your own life and answering the following questions:

Am I content with my lot in life? __________

Am I pursuing the Lord and my relationship with Him above all other pursuits? __________

If not, be honest enough to write down what you are pursuing. Confess it as a form of idolatry and ask the Lord to help you pursue Him and allow Him to satisfy your longing heart.

____

____

____

____

____

____

____

____

MEMORY VERSE
"Turn away my eyes from looking at worthless things, and revive me in Your way. Establish Your word to Your servant who is devoted to fearing You." Psalm 119:37, 38

". . . what does the LORD require of you But to do justly, To love mercy, And to walk humbly with your God?"

Micah 6:8

BETTER THAN . . .

The Serious Side of Life

DAY FIVE

Ecclesiastes 7:1–10

As I look back on my childhood, some of my fondest memories are reflections of our family camping trips and vacations. It was a time for my parents to get away and relax and a time for my brother and me to take a road trip and spend the week somewhere other than home. Unfortunately, my dad and mom always thought the vacation was going to turn out very differently than it actually did. They had a very strange equation for the perfect vacation: Leave Point A, take a coffee can so they wouldn't have to stop, eat packed peanut butter-and-jelly sandwiches on the way, and then arrive at Point B, where they would finally get to relax. I'm sure it would have all turned out as they wanted it to if they hadn't had two children in the backseat fussing, fighting, and asking a million questions all the way there. ("Are we there yet?") Not one of our vacations ever turned out exactly as they had expected, yet somehow, they enjoyed it and were thankful they were able to go.

Solomon has taken us on a trip from Point A to Point B, and just like my parents' vacation, it's been anything but what we expected. He has taken us down some very sobering and seemingly pessimistic roads, showing us the stark reality of how vain it is to live solely for this life, under the sun. However, he has also given us some really sound advice about enjoying this life as a gift from God and trusting the Lord to make all things beautiful in His time. It may not have been what we expected, but I pray you've enjoyed the journey so far.

Up to this point we've been blessed to glean wisdom from Solomon the Preacher as he allows his life experiences to become lessons for ours. But he's not finished yet. As we continue in our study of Ecclesiastes, we will find Solomon beginning to change his approach in conveying his wisdom. Previously, he used many verses to give us his take on specific topics, but now we are going to hear from another Solomon—the same Solomon who wrote much of the book of Proverbs—with what seem to be random tidbits of wisdom. Just as he did in Proverbs, Solomon will now take us from one thought to the next within a few verses. It may seem as though he's all over the place in his writings, but isn't that how we live our lives, all over the place? We go from one place to the next; one decision to the next; one event to the next; and one plan to the next. So, buckle up, sweet friends, we're going to take a ride through the next few chapters of Ecclesiastes. Prepare yourself for random stops and unexpected turns.

"A good name is better than precious ointment, . . ."

Ecclesiastes 7:1

📖 Begin by reading Ecclesiastes 7:1–10. How many times does Solomon use the expression "better than"? __________

As we read we find that Solomon gives us a series of thoughts diametrically opposed to the way we would generally think. He begins by telling us that a good name (a good reputation) is *better than* precious perfume. In Solomon's day, perfume was quite rare and therefore very costly. It was just as rare and costly in New Testament times. John 12:3 tells us of a woman named Mary who poured a pound of very expensive and fragrant oil on Jesus' feet. In verse 5 we learn that the value of that sixteen ounces of perfume was three hundred denarii—the equivalent of about a year's wages.

In ancient Jewish culture, those who were wealthy enough to purchase this valuable perfume would seal it in a beautiful box, then set it in a safe place where nothing could get into it and contaminate it. Any contaminant could cause its sweet fragrance to be spoiled.

Like that sweet perfume, our reputations should also be relentlessly guarded. *Who we are and who others perceive us to be is intrinsically linked to the way in which we conduct ourselves.* We need to be careful not to allow anything in our lives that would contaminate our reputation. The decisions we make can cause our lives to be like sweet-smelling perfume—or a foul-smelling stench. A good name is not something we can easily obtain; it takes time to earn it. It can't be bought, but it can be sold. Unfortunately, it only takes a moment in time to ruin a reputation that took a lifetime to build. Many have sold their reputations for a few moments of pleasure; for a few extra dollars; for a few minutes of fame. It takes years to build a good reputation, minutes to lose it . . . and a lifetime to attempt to gain it back. Most never do. So when Solomon tells us a good name is better than precious ointment, he is packing a powerful illustrative punch with the use of perfume.

You can guard your reputation by avoiding certain people, places, thoughts, and events. If you are facing a temptation that could contaminate your reputation, please tell what you need to avoid in order to gain victory over your temptation.

"A good name is to be chosen rather than great riches . . ."

Proverbs 22:1

____

____

____

____

____

____

Sweet friend, we were not meant to wage war on our own. If you are engaged in a battle to protect your reputation, I want to encourage to you find a faithful friend who will stand in the gap for you and be a dependable accountability and prayer partner. Remember the lesson we learned in Ecclesiastes 4:9. Two are definitely better than one.

In contrast, your reputation is built more on how you behave than just the choice to avoid certain things. Your conduct exhibits your character and reinforces your reputation. So it's important to be who you say you are or you'll be known as a fake trying to pull off some type of pseudo-Christianity, giving the world an excuse to reject Christ because they reject your version of Christianity. "Oh, Lord, never allow me to be someone's excuse for not receiving You!"

As we move on in our study today, we find that in verse 2 Solomon tells us that the day of one's death is better than the day of one's birth. He continues as he declares that it is better to go to the house of mourning than it is to go to a party. I'm very thankful Solomon didn't stop there. He goes on to tell us, "It is the end of every man and the wise will take it to heart."

If you've ever been to a funeral you know it's a place where people come face-to-face with their own mortality. It is there many decide to make changes in their lives before their own eulogy is given. It is there the wise man has the opportunity to *take it to heart*.

A dear friend of mine died several years ago. He touched so many lives that people stood in the rain for hours to pay their respects at his viewing. The funeral had to be held in the biggest church on our side of town in order to accommodate the thousands of people who attended. I remember thinking, *I want to make a difference as he did.* He had a good reputation . . . he guarded it . . . and the living took it to heart.

📖 Now look at verses 3 and 4 and paraphrase what Solomon is saying.

____

____

____

____

These verses may be a little hard to understand in light of Proverbs 17:22, which tells us, *"A merry heart does good, like medicine"* (NKJV), and John 10:10, which declares that Jesus came to give us an abundant life. So how does all this line up with Ecclesiastes 7:3, 4? To gain a better understanding, let's turn to the Word.

📖 Please read 2 Corinthians 7:10.
What does godly sorrow produce?

____

____

What does it lead to?

____

____

We can't really enjoy this life apart from knowing Christ, and we can't be saved unless we are first willing to take a good hard look at ourselves, allowing the Spirit of God to expose our sinfulness. It is then that godly sorrow produces the repentance necessary for salvation.

📖 Now read James 4:6–10.
What does verse 9 tell us to do?

____

____

Our readiness to repent is absolutely essential to living a godly, victorious, and abundant life.

Repentance is part of the process of salvation, but it is also necessary to maintain a life that honors God. Our readiness to repent is absolutely essential to living a godly, victorious, and abundant life.

In Ecclesiastes 7:4–6 Solomon moves on to the wisdom that comes from listening to and acting upon wise correction. We talked about this when we studied Ecclesiastes 4:9–16, but it never hurts to be reminded. We need to surround ourselves with wise friends in order to avail ourselves of wise counsel.

Have you ever heard crackling thorns under a pot? They make a lot of noise but they don't really accomplish anything. That's what the songs of fools are like: really loud, but they don't really accomplish anything. The songs and laughter of fools may be a distraction from the realities of life, but they are still empty. Although it may sometimes be difficult to listen to wise counsel, at least it's noise with a purpose. At least it can encourage us to live as we should.

📖 Now read verse 7. What do oppression and bribery do?

____

____

Oppression takes away a man's reason; bribery takes away a man's integrity. Notice that Solomon doesn't give us a comparison here. In the ten verses we are studying today, he tells of seven things that are better than others. In verse 7, he doesn't make a comparison, he just makes a simple statement because neither is better than the other. Both oppression and bribery exact a heavy toll on those they affect.

📖 Now read verses 8 and 9 and fill in the blanks.
The ____________ is better than the _______________.
The ____________ is better than the _______________.
Don't be eager in your heart to be _____________. Why?

____

____

____

I began to understand what Solomon was saying in verse 8 when we went to the mission field. We were filled with dreams of and plans for what we thought we were going to do there. The Lord used us . . . but not at all as we expected. When we begin something, we are filled with excitement and anticipation of all the possibilities. But when all is said and done, we can look back and see how the Lord had His hand on us every step of the way. We find that His plan for the ultimate outcome is much better than we could have dreamed; we learn from our successes and our failures. Even when things don't turn out as we plan, we can understand why Solomon said the end is better than the beginning.

He also said patience is better than pride. Now, in our Christian circles it's very easy to agree with this statement, but it runs contrary to all this world teaches us. We are to look out for number 1 . . . we are to fight for our rights . . . we are to stand up for ourselves, fight our way to the top . . . we are to make ourselves shine. But as a Christian, I'm to die to self, I'm to put other's needs before my own, I've given up my rights, and my desire is to let Jesus shine through me and to point others to Him. That takes patience; that takes self-control; that takes walking in the Spirit and allowing the fruit of the Spirit to be displayed in my life.

"But let patience have its perfect work, that you may be perfect and complete, lacking nothing."

James 1:4

Patience is better than pride because it is part of the foundation of a good reputation. Those who become angry quickly only prove they don't possess a patient spirit. We actually undermine our own reputations when we choose not to control ourselves.

📖 As we conclude today's lesson, read Ecclesiastes 7:10. Take note of how Solomon uses the expression "better than" in a negative sense. Then paraphrase what he is saying.

____

____

____

____

Solomon advises us it's not wise to spend our lives looking back on the good ol' days. We don't live in the past . . . we live now. We can't change our past . . . we can only change now.

Have you ever been around someone who devotes most of her conversation to talking about events that occurred years ago? Like a broken record, it's as if they were stuck in time and can't get past a specific period locked in their minds. Life may be harder now, but we can't allow present difficulties to cause us to mentally and emotionally retreat to a day when things seemed much easier. Today's study echoes yesterday's lesson, teaching us that contentment with our lot in life enables us to live today to its fullest. We need to accept the lot God has given us in life, and live where we are . . . now.

Take a moment to answer the following questions:

Do I have a tendency to live in the past? __________
Am I facing something today I'd rather hide with thoughts of yesterday? ________

"Do not say, 'Why were the former days better than these?' . . ."
Ecclesiastes 7:10

Paul tells us in Philippians 3:13, 14, "*. . . but one thing I do: forgetting what lies behind and reaching forward to what lies ahead, I press on toward the goal for the prize of the upward call of God in Christ Jesus.*"

We've covered a lot of "better thans" today and I pray that this lesson has served as a reminder of the necessity of guarding your reputation as a valuable gift. I pray that we will all better understand our responsibility for each choice we make and our need to take a serious look at our lives, evaluating the areas that need to be brought into line with the way God calls us to live. After all—that's what really matters most, isn't it?!

MEMORY VERSE
"Turn away my eyes from looking at worthless things, and revive me in Your way. Establish Your word to Your servant who is devoted to fearing You." Psalm 119:37, 38

MEMORY TIP
Recite your verse to someone in your small group and let her read it to you also.

5

Having a Proper Perspective

The way we handle life (or the way we allow life to handle us) is often determined by our personal perspective. This week we will see that the proper perspective has the potential to clarify what we value, determine how we will respond to authority, influence whether we enjoy this life, and establish how we deal with ever-changing realities.

"For the grace of God that brings salvation has appeared to all men, teaching us that, denying ungodliness and worldly lusts, we should live soberly, righteously, and godly in this present age, looking for that blessed hope and glorious appearing of our great God and Savior Jesus Christ." Titus 2:11–13

"Who among you is wise and understanding? . . ."
James 3:13

DAY 1 The Value of Wisdom
DAY 2 Understanding Authority
DAY 3 Permission to Enjoy Life
DAY 4 Ah, the Good Life!
DAY 5 The Inconsistencies of Life

MEMORY VERSE
"Who among you is wise and understanding? Let him show by his good behavior his deeds in the gentleness of wisdom." James 3:13 (NASB)

Having a Proper Perspective

DAY ONE

THE VALUE OF WISDOM

Ecclesiastes 7:11–29

I remember that not long after I turned 40, the words on the page became a little fuzzy. Although I had to pull my head back a little in order to read my Bible, I was bound and determined *not* to buy reading glasses. You might say I was in denial because I was very content to continue to pull my head back and stretch my arms out every morning. I called it *my morning stretch.* Finally, the time came when that didn't work any more and I had to make a choice. I could either admit that I couldn't see clearly and do what was necessary to fix my problem, or I could just quit reading. Of course, I broke down and bought the glasses because the ability to read is essential for me.

Many times we approach life in the same way. We think things will be okay; we just deal with the circumstances, adjusting ourselves just enough to get by. But all the while we're actually in denial of the fact that we just don't have the wisdom to see things clearly. We need the reading glasses of God's Word and the bifocals of God's wisdom to see things clearly. God's wisdom helps eliminate the fuzziness of life and enables us to make wise decisions.

Throughout this study we have been reminded that Solomon was the wisest man who ever lived. However, today we are going to take a closer look at wisdom: We're going to learn what it is, and how it is essential to our lives.

So, what exactly is *wisdom?* The *American Heritage Dictionary* defines it as "the understanding of what is true, right, or lasting; common sense, good judgment." But let's look at what the Bible says about wisdom.

"The fear of the LORD is the instruction of wisdom, . . ."

Proverbs 15:33

📖 Please read Psalm 111:10 and Proverbs 9:10. What do these verses say about wisdom?

____

____

____

The phrase "beginning of wisdom," found in both verses, means, "The first essential or prerequisite; the choice part of wisdom." In other words, the prerequisite for, the essential element of, wisdom is an authentic and reverential fear of God. So, if you and I ever expect to gain wisdom, we must first sincerely revere and fear God. That's where wisdom begins.

Psalm 111:10 takes us a step further in its explanation of wisdom. It says, *"A good understanding have all those who do His commandments."*

You see, wisdom is not only *knowing* what is right, it is displayed by *doing* what is right.

📖 Please read Ecclesiastes 7:11–29 and fill in the blanks.

Verse 11: Wisdom is ______________________________ and ______________________________.

Verse 12: Wisdom is ______________________________ and ______________________________.

Verse 19: Wisdom ____
____.

Throughout these verses Solomon very aptly conveys the value of wisdom. In today's lesson, Solomon will be all over the place as he unleashes his wisdom concerning a variety of issues. In verses 11 and 12 he begins by comparing the value of wisdom with the value of an inheritance. The Amplified Bible says, *"Wisdom is as good as an inheritance, yes more excellent it is for those [the living] who see the sun. For wisdom is a defense even as money is a defense, but the excellency of knowledge is that wisdom shields and preserves the life of him who has it."*

Solomon was a man who had it all, but he wanted us to understand that the value (wealth) of wisdom far outweighs the benefits of a large inheritance because wisdom enables us to see life clearly and to live with the right perspective. Unfortunately, all we gain through an inheritance can be lost, stolen, or squandered in a moment of time. So, in Solomon's discourse on wisdom, he begins by reminding us it's priceless! Walking in wisdom means having clarity, peace, and integrity in any given situation. You see, dear one, we may gain a lot of wealth in this world, but if we don't have the wisdom to manage it properly, if we don't have the wisdom to put its value in the proper perspective, we could lose it all in the blink of an eye. Even worse than that, we could compromise our integrity by trying to hold on to it.

So let's take a look at wisdom through Solomon's eyes. As we've already seen, verses 11 and 12 teach us how to view our finances. Whether we have received a large inheritance or not, we need to maintain a proper perspective on our finances. Money may be necessary, but it can't buy life, health, or heaven. Wisdom shields and preserves our lives because it helps us make the right decisions in the circumstances we face.

Now look at verses 13 and 14. They remind us of our need to have the proper understanding of God's sovereignty. What God does . . . He does. We can not undo what He has done. He is ultimately in complete control. He is God and He sovereignly rules the universe. There is much wisdom in being content with the road on which we often find ourselves as we rest in the Lord. It's not always easy: Some roads are more difficult than others, some seasons more enjoyable than others, but no matter how hard the journey, our Loving Father has promised, *"Never will I leave you; never will I forsake you"* (Hebrews 13:5 NIV). He has told us others have shared in the same trials and that His presence will be a very evident reality in even our most difficult circumstances. We can rest in Him.

In verse 15, Solomon encourages us to view the unfairness of life through the eyes of wisdom. We've all faced certain circumstances that prompted us to say, "This just isn't right . . . it isn't fair!" However, when we gaze through the glasses of wisdom, we're able to clearly see there is a day of reckoning for each of us and what may seem unfair from our earthly perspective will be made irrefutably right in eternity. We may not understand why things happen the way they do, under the sun, but we are reminded we are just pilgrims on this planet. There is a day coming when the senseless will make sense and our understanding will be complete.

". . . Is there unrighteousness with God? Certainly not!"

Romans 9:14

Now turn your attention to verses 16 through 18. Here we are given the wisdom to have the right view of ourselves. We are admonished not to be self-righteous or "too smart for our own good," and not to be foolishly wicked. It's interesting to know that self-righteousness and wickedness both stem from pride.

📖 Please read Romans 12:3 and paraphrase it here.

____

____

____

____

When we think we're so righteous and so wise we only reveal how proud and foolish we really are.

Let's face it, dear one, we all have a propensity for pride. When we think we're *so* righteous and *so* wise we only reveal how proud and foolish we really are. And, as Ecclesiastes 7:17 warns us, the wicked often die an untimely death as a result of their foolish choices. Whether one is proud and foolish or wicked and foolish, both live and die as fools.

Verse 18 returns us to a life of balance acquired by an authentic and reverential fear of God. When we examine the issues of life that we all face on a daily basis, it is the fear of God that provides us with the wisdom to avoid the extremes of either side and to live a balanced life in an unbalanced world.

Many times we face circumstances capable of *breaking* us if we are not strong enough, or *making* us if we will walk in God's wisdom. In verse 19 we find we are empowered beyond belief and beyond understanding when we walk in the wisdom of God. Our ability to stand when our world is crashing in around us is derived from the wisdom of the Living God. His counsel stands—and so do we when we choose to seek His wisdom, spending time in His Word and time in prayer, and act on the wisdom He bestows to each willing heart.

📖 Please take a moment to read Ecclesiastes 7:20–22.

I remember one day when my husband was looking for something he used for recording and he thought either our son, D.J., or I had put it somewhere. He wasn't a happy camper as we continually pleaded our innocence. After a few hours of time spent in hostile territory he came out of the studio with a sheepish smile as he reluctantly admitted he had found his coveted item in the same bag he had put it in a few days earlier. We're all guilty of blaming others for that which we have done. The mirror is the best place to start when we seek to place blame. Solomon uses these three verses to remind us there are no perfect people. We are a fallen race . . . we all sin. We sin against God and we sin against one another. We've all been hurt by the careless or even calculated words and deeds of others. But we've also been the perpetrator of the same painfully foolish acts. Dear one, let's let these verses serve as a reminder the next time someone blows it and says something they shouldn't say: We need to be women who are quick to extend mercy in the same way we would want extended to us. (We might just need it sooner than we think!)

📖 Please read verses 23 through 25.

I wish I were smarter. I even pray, "Lord, make me smarter . . . make me wiser than I am." I'm well aware I'm not the brightest bulb on the tree, but these verses comfort me and remind me there is wisdom in knowing there are just some things we are never going to be wise enough to understand . . . and that's okay. There are times when life leaves us without answers. There are circumstances we just can't explain. We've all been asked questions such as, "Why did God take my baby?" "Why did my uncle sexually abuse me?" "Why didn't my mother get saved before she died?" "Why was I born with this disability?" "Why does God allow Satan to tempt people?" "Why is my husband so hard to live with?"

These are all questions crying out for an answer, but the only answer we can offer is, "I don't know!" We *really don't know everything* and if we pretend we do, we stand guilty of doing what it says in verse 16 . . . being overly (pretentiously) wise. Solomon lets us off the hook in these verses as he tells us he tried to understand some things far beyond his human wisdom. The wisest man to ever live was not ashamed to say, "There are just some things that are beyond my understanding." If he was wise enough to know his limitations, then we should not be ashamed to also say, "I just don't know!"

📖 Now let's take a look at verses 26 through 29.

In these verses we are instructed to view our relationships through the eyes of wisdom. Solomon begins by using an illustration of an adulterous woman: one who seduces a man, entangling him and capturing him in her net of sin and destruction. Unfortunately, Solomon was all too familiar with that type of woman. After all, he had hundreds of women at his disposal. As we studied in Week 1, many of those women penetrated his heart with the deceptive hook of idolatry.

Let's face it—when we read these verses, specifically verse 28—we may think Solomon was a woman-hater, but we know from his other writings that that wasn't the case at all. In fact, he spoke very highly of virtuous and godly women (Proverbs 5:18–20; 12:4; 14:1; 18:22; 31:10–31; and the entire book of Song of Solomon). Unfortunately, his own experience made him well aware of what a seductress was capable of doing to a man. Solomon is trying to relay the wisdom he gained through personal failure to all who will listen. His warning is obviously directed to men, but we women have to be careful to put up our own personal boundaries in areas of temptation, as well.

All right, now it's time for me to play mom to all the single ladies reading this Bible study. Beware of the wolves in gentlemen's clothing. The guys who pretend to love Jesus as they creep into the churches trying to woo a wife. However, these chameleon men change their colors the moment she says, "I do." How often I have heard the heart's cry of a woman who married a man who turned out to be someone she really didn't even know!

Beware of the wolves in gentlemen's clothing.

God gives us the wisdom we need to really evaluate the people we choose to be involved with, but we have to heed God's warnings. That whole don't be *"unequally yoked"* thing (2 Corinthians 6:14 KJV) is actually for our good, not to keep something good from us. Our response to God's wisdom should be a resounding, "Yes! I trust You, Lord, in all my ways!" Allow the Lord to give you the wisdom to see your relationships clearly.

Notice in verse 29 Solomon levels the playing field and makes it clear both men and women have the uncanny ability to mess things up. Here, wisdom teaches us to see our own condition before a holy God . . . to know our own depravity . . . to understand our need. The Amplified Bible says it this way: *"God made man upright, but they [men and women] have sought out many devices [for evil]."* Our hearts are truly desperately wicked. There is none that does good . . . no not one. There is none that seeks after God. We are all in desperate need and Jesus is our only hope. Our condition is this: God made us upright, but we have all sought out many schemes. How great is our propensity to desire or do that which is wrong!

Oh, that we would be brought to the end of ourselves and throw ourselves at the Savior's feet, asking for mercy, forgiveness, and grace! When we come face-to-face with who we really are in the deepest recesses of our hearts, when we understand our need, it is wisdom that brings us to the place where we can repent and surrender ourselves to the Living God. Sincere and reverential fear is where wisdom begins!

📖 Below I have included some verses to help deepen your biblical understanding of wisdom. Please take this opportunity to look each of them up and fill in the blanks.

"And to man He said, 'Behold, the fear of the Lord, that is wisdom; And to depart from evil is understanding.'"

Job 28:28 (NASB)

Job 28:28 (NASB): *"And to man He said, 'Behold, the fear of the Lord, that is wisdom; And to depart from evil is understanding.'"*

What is *wisdom?*

____

____

What is *understanding?*

____

____

Proverbs 2:6 (NASB): *"For the LORD gives wisdom; From His mouth come knowledge and understanding;"*

Who gives wisdom, knowledge, and understanding?_______________

Psalm 90:12 (NASB): *"So teach us to number our days, That we may present to You a heart of wisdom."*

What is the benefit of understanding how to number our days?

____

____

Proverbs 1:7 (NASB): *"The fear of the LORD is the beginning of knowledge; Fools despise wisdom and instruction."*

What do fools despise?_______________________________

Proverbs 8:11 (NASB): *"For wisdom is better than jewels; And all desirable things cannot compare with her."*

What is the value of wisdom?

____

James 1:5 (NASB): *"But if any of you lacks wisdom, let him ask of God, who gives to all generously and without reproach, and it will be given to him."*

How do we acquire wisdom?

___

Today, we have had the privilege of gleaning wisdom not only from Solomon, but from the Living God. In His Word, He has revealed to us what wisdom is, what it is worth, how to obtain it, and how to apply it in various real-life circumstances. Remember, wisdom is not what we know, but it's how we live in light of what we know to be true. I pray, dear one, that you will truly grasp the ability that is ours as children of God to see things clearly and to live wisely.

Wisdom is how we live in light of what we know to be true.

Please don't forget to start memorizing this week's verse!
"Who among you is wise and understanding?
Let him show by his good behavior his deeds in the gentleness of wisdom." James 3:13

MEMORY TIP
Write your memory verse on a 3x5 card and tape it to your monthly calendar in the kitchen. Every day when you look at your calendar, review your memory verse.

Having a Proper Perspective

DAY TWO

UNDERSTANDING AUTHORITY

Ecclesiastes 8:1–9

It has been said one of the greatest evidences of character is the ability to submit to authority. Perhaps that's because submission requires humility, and humility is without question one of the most noble qualities a person can exhibit. As we look at today's verses in Ecclesiastes we will find Solomon's admonition to each of us to submit to those in governmental authority. Then we're going to take this opportunity to study the biblical principle of submitting to and obeying the other authority figures in our lives.

Please begin today's lesson by reading Ecclesiastes 8:1–9 in the New Living Translation:

> *"How wonderful to be wise, to analyze and interpret things. Wisdom lights up a person's face, softening its harshness. Obey the king since you vowed to God that you would. Don't try to avoid doing your duty, and don't stand with those who plot evil, for the king can do whatever he wants. His command is backed by great power. No one can resist or question it. Those who obey him will not be punished. Those who are wise will find a time and a way to do what is right, for there is a time and a way for everything, even when a person is in trouble. Indeed, how can people avoid what they don't know is going to happen? None of us can hold back our spirit from departing. None of us has the power to prevent the day of our death. There is no escaping that obligation, that dark battle. And in the face of death, wickedness will certainly not rescue the wicked. I have thought deeply about all that goes on here under the sun, where people have the power to hurt each other."*

Notice that verse 1 speaks of the wonder that wisdom produces in one's life. But the second part of that verse goes on to tell us wisdom not only affects the way we see things and the way we live, it also affects our appearance. Wisdom is a powerful tool available to God's children, and one of its many benefits is found in the way it can bring a special glow to our faces. It has the power to soften the lines brought about by a difficult life. Life isn't always easy, but when we walk in wisdom, we can reflect a soft glow regardless of how hard our circumstances really are. So, ladies, if you're looking for a surgery-free facelift, get in the Word, pursue God's wisdom and let the glowing begin!

In verses 2 through 6, Solomon urges us to be wise enough to submit to the authority of the king. Now, as a king, he was very much aware of his own power and knew that it was in the best interest of the whole kingdom that people submit to his authority. He understood his power, but he also understood that with great power also comes great responsibility. He himself was guilty of oppressing people (1 Kings 9:21; 2 Chronicles 8:8), so he knew the danger of foolishly disobeying the king.

"Remind them to be subject to rulers and authorities, to obey, to be ready for every good work,"

Titus 3:1

Submission is one of those words that has the tendency to make you wince. In its basic definition it means "yielding oneself to authority." It actually comes from the Greek word *hupottaso,* which is a military term meaning "to rank oneself under another." It includes the concept of obeying those you have ranked yourself under. We do it all the time without even thinking about it. We yield to stop signs and school crossings. We yield to speed limits and civil law. We submit to authorities at our jobs, pastors at our churches, teachers in our schools, and policemen on the streets. Sometimes submission comes without resistance. However, it seems that when we attach the word *submission* to our role as a wife, and when we read the biblical mandate to be submissive to our husbands, resentment has a way of rearing its ugly head.

Now that we have a basic idea of what *submission* means, I want to be sure we all understand what it does *not* mean. It does not mean we are less intelligent or less important. It does not mean we are a doormat or that we're to be dominated. It just means someone has to lead the way and the Lord has ordained or allowed certain people to do just that.

Truthfully, the concept of submission to authority is not very difficult to explain, because it's not really hard to understand—it's just hard to do. It is important we remember that our willingness to submit to our earthly authorities is a very good reflection of our willingness to submit to our heavenly Father.

In Ecclesiastes 8:2, Solomon links obedience to the king with a vow made to God. It most likely refers to the oath Solomon had made when he became king. Since we studied in Week 4 the seriousness of keeping our vows, we understand how crucial it is—even when it means submitting to authority.

Let's take a few minutes and look at the subject of submission a little more closely.

🕮 Please read the following verses and answer the questions. Please take note of the order in which I have placed them. Our line of authority and our submission to it follows the order in which I have placed them.

Ephesians 5:24; James 4:7
According to these verses, to whom are we to submit?

husbands
God

If we have a problem submitting to God, then we will have a problem submitting to other forms of authority. If we have no problem submitting to God, then we should have no problem submitting to other forms of authority.

Ephesians 5:22, 23; Colossians 3:18; Titus 2:4, 5
According to these verses, to whom are we to submit and why?

husbands. Husbands are heads of the wives. Jesus is the head of the church.
Do not bring shame to God

Hebrews 13:17; 1 Peter 5:5
According to these verses, to whom are we to submit and why?

spiritual leaders. They are accountable to God.
Serve with humility

Ephesians 5:21
According to this verse, to whom are we to submit?

One another out of reverence for Christ.

"Honor all people. Love the brotherhood. Fear God. Honor the king."

I Peter 2:17

Romans 13:1–5; Titus 3:1
According to these verses, to whom are we to submit?

Governing authorities

Ephesians 6:5; 1 Peter 2:18 (We may not have masters, but if we work, we have a boss or supervisor).
According to these verses, to whom are we to submit?

Slaves obey masters

Look back on those we are required to submit to and circle the most difficult for you.

Remember, the concept of submission is really quite simple—the problem comes when we are faced with a situation in which we have to actually do it.

Many times we find it hard to submit because our pride gets in the way. Submission requires humility, and we are given the perfect example of both submission and humility in the Lord Jesus Christ. Let's look at the example He has given us.

In Luke 2:51, what characteristic did Jesus display? Submission

In John 8:28, 29 and 5:30, what characteristic is evident in Jesus' life? Humility

He does what God tells Him to do

📖 Please read Philippians 2:5–10 and explain how Jesus displayed humility and submission.

Eventhough He is God, He gave up his position and obeyed God. He died for everyone. Everyone will obey Him

There is a principle in Philippians 2:5–10 that is true for us as well as it was for Jesus. You see, our heavenly Father will lift us up if we choose to humble ourselves and submit to His authority (James 4:10; 1 Peter 5:5–7). Obviously, we won't experience the same exaltation as Jesus did when He was seated at the right hand of the Father and given a name above every name, but our heavenly Father promises to lift us up if we will humble ourselves under His mighty hand.

When we submit to authority, it demonstrates that we understand the sovereignty of God and that all authority is given by God. Consider the example Jesus conveys when He was facing a certain and painful death. While being questioned by the Roman governor, Pilate, Jesus stood silent. In John 19:10, 11 (NASB), notice what Jesus says when Pilate rebukes Him for not answering his questions: *So Pilate said to Him, "You do not speak to me? Do You not know that I have authority to release You, and I have authority to crucify You?" Jesus answered, "You would have no authority over Me, unless it had been given you from above; for this reason he who delivered Me to you has the greater sin."*

We are to obey God rather than man.

There are times when those in authority over us may try to coerce us to do things contrary to God's Word or God's principles. In such a dilemma, we find the simple solution in Acts 4:18–20 and Acts 5:29: We are to obey God rather than man.

So the next time you are given the opportunity to submit to someone in a position of authority, look at it from a biblical perspective and as an opportunity to please God.

The final verse in today's lesson is Ecclesiastes 8:9, where Solomon, from a kingly perspective, gives us a final warning about submitting to authority. He reminds us there are times we need to submit to those in authority because they wield the strong arm of power to harm us. Many submit to their employers because they don't want to lose their jobs; many submit to civil authorities because they don't want to be put in jail; however, in Solomon's day, many submitted to authority because the king had the power to decree death.

As we finish today's lesson, I pray you will evaluate your own life and your willingness to submit to the authorities God has placed in your life. If you are struggling in any area of submission, please remember, dear one, that your willingness to submit to your earthly authorities is a good reflection of your willingness to submit to your heavenly Father.

MEMORY VERSE
"Who among you is wise and understanding? Let him show by his good behavior his deeds in the gentleness of wisdom." James 3:13 (NASB)

MEMORY TIP
Say your memory verse three times in the morning and three times before bed.

Having a Proper Perspective

DAY THREE

PERMISSION TO ENJOY LIFE:

Ecclesiastes 8:10–17

I'm sure I've said this before, but one of my favorite things to do is laugh. I laugh at myself, I laugh at my husband, my children, my dog, my circumstances, and my mistakes. Although I take my relationship with the Lord very seriously, I tend to look for humor in almost every aspect of my life. I've lived long enough to understand we only get to do this thing called *life* once, so we need to live it fervently for the Lord and enjoy the journey along the way.

As I began to study for today's lesson, I was thrilled when I realized Solomon was actually taking the time to give us permission to enjoy this life. Now, I realize he has made this statement several times before, but this particular time it seemed to jump off the page of Scripture and land with a happy face in my heart.

Throughout our study of Ecclesiastes, we have basically taken a verse-by-verse, precept-by-precept approach. Today I would like to do something different. Today, we're going to do a little moonwalking through our verses as we begin with verses 16 and 17 and walk our way backward to verse 10. Now bear with me through this unexpected process and I think you'll enjoy the change of pace.

"... The Creator of the ends of the earth, Neither faints nor is weary. His understanding is unsearchable."
Isaiah 40:28

📖 Begin by reading Ecclesiastes 8:16, 17, then summarize these verses in your own words.

People worry to much. They need to know everything

You may remember that Solomon made a similar statement in Ecclesiastes 3:11 when he said no one can *"find out the work which God has done from the beginning even to the end."* In all his wisdom, in all his attempts to understand everything about everything, Solomon came to the very brilliant conclusion that his knowledge and wisdom were extremely limited. You see, it's wonderful to have discernment and insight; it's a blessing to be wise. In Ecclesiastes 7:25, Solomon writes that he determined, he gave his heart, to know wisdom, but in all his determination he understood there are just some things in life we will never have the capacity to understand. There is so much Solomon couldn't even begin to comprehend about God. And so it is with each of us.

It is actually comforting to know we serve a God beyond our comprehension. He is God . . . and we are not. He holds the universe in place; He rotates the earth on its axis; He prohibits the oceans from overflowing the land; He knows the stars by name; He knows the number of hairs on each of our heads; He knows our deepest desires and our innermost fears; He is infinite; He is holy; His ways are always perfect and right. He is God! How could He possibly be reduced to the size of our understanding?

In John Wesley's *Explanatory Notes on the Whole Bible,* he says of verse 17, "No man, though ever so wise, is able fully and perfectly to understand these things. And therefore, it is best for man not to perplex himself with endless enquiries, but quietly to submit to God's will and providence, and to live in the fear of God, and the comfortable enjoyment of His blessing."[7]

You see, sometimes we face things we don't understand in this life . . . things that throw us for a loop. But it is very reassuring to know we serve a real God who really is in control of a world that seems so out of control. It helps to know that when things don't make sense we can trust that God will make sense of it all. Maybe not today, maybe not even in our lifetime, but one day, we will know and understand just as we have been known and understood by the Lord (1 Corinthians 15:12).

". . . How unsearchable are His judgments and His ways past finding out!"
Romans 11:33

📖 Turn in your Bible to Isaiah 40:13, then Romans 11:33–35. After reading these passages, write out what you believe to be the overall concept.

God is too powerful for us to understand.

You see, dear one, we can either strain our brains and lose sleep trying to figure God out, or we can rest in the fact that He alone is God . . . and we are not. We can't understand everything that goes on in this world, just like we can't understand all there is to know about God. But we can trust God and we can trust God's character as we walk down the pathway of life. In fact, our ability to rest in the sovereignty of God helps us to enjoy this life we all live, under the sun.

📖 Now it's time to move on to verse 15. After you read it, please answer the following questions:

Do you really consider yourself someone who enjoys this life? Sometimes

Describe the last time you belly-laughed.

Probably around my sister

What are some of the things that prohibit you from really enjoying the life God has given you?

Being angry about things not going the way I would like for them to go

Compare Ecclesiastes 2:24; 3:13, 22; 5:18. What does each of these verses seem to say?

Have fun in everything we do. God wants us to have fun and enjoy all He has given us

Earlier, I said this verse just jumped off the page into my heart. Well, I believe that may have been Solomon's intention. You see, if you look at verse 15, it begins with the statement, *"So I commended pleasure."* The word *commended* actually comes from the Hebrew word *shabach*, which stems from the primitive root meaning "to address in a loud tone." I can almost picture Solomon crying through the corridors of time: "Enjoy yourself . . . really . . . it's okay. Live, love, and laugh . . . have a blast. It will help you through the hard times this life will throw your way."

Some theologians believe that the call in verse 15 to enjoy life is actually just a comment to those who live life under the sun apart from God. They find verse 15 to mean that if we are going to live life under the sun (apart from God), then we need to eat, drink, and be merry because it's all there is to look forward to. But as I was reading through various commentaries and studying the context of some of these words, I came to believe that Solomon was not limiting it to the godless, but to all who live and breathe on Planet Earth. At the end of verse 15, he calls us to remember that this life we all live under the sun is a gift from God. Life can only be enjoyed with God in the picture.

". . . nor to trust in uncertain riches but in the living God, who gives us richly all things to enjoy."

I Timothy 6:17

Sometimes laughter is one of the best therapies for the difficult days we face, and Solomon knew that. His position in life caused him to look at things from a very sober and apparently pessimistic point of view. He knew life was hard; he understood that everyone faces trials and tribulations—even the king. His role as king only magnified his need to see the lighter side of things. He understood that laughter was good for the soul. In Proverbs 17:22, Solomon wrote, *"A joyful heart is good medicine . . ."* In fact, science has proved Solomon's proverb to be true. According to Dr. Lee Berk and Dr. Stanley Tan of Loma Linda University, when we laugh, several chemicals and hormones are produced that actually boost our immune system. Laughter has positive effects on our respiratory and circulatory systems and not only has been proven to lower blood pressure, but is also very good for people with diabetes and provides a host of other physical benefits.[8] Laughter truly is good . . . like a medicine!

APPLY Now, it's time to take a minute and evaluate your laugh meter. Do you look at life as if you were (check all that apply):

_____ Somber Sarah
__✓__ Sulky Susie
__✓__ Serious Sandy
_____ Lighthearted Louise
_____ Laughing Linda
__✓__ Negative Nellie
_____ Positive Pam
__✓__ Pessimistic Priscilla
_____ Optimistic Opal
__✓__ Grumpy Gertrude

Now do something else interesting. Give permission to someone you're close with to check off all the characteristics they believe apply to you. Then compare your responses.

Life is too short to spend it looking at all the bad things that have happened to you.

Recently I heard someone say, "Life is too short to spend it looking at all the bad things that have happened to you. You need to focus on all the good things that have happened to you instead." Now that's good advice! I will come back to this point at the conclusion of today's lesson, but first we need to review verses 10 though 14.

📖 Begin by reading verses 10 through 14 and summarizing the meaning of each verse.

Verse 10

~~Money doesn't buy happiness~~

Verse 11

~~More money, more problems. Be careful who your friends are~~

Verse 12

~~Work for what you have~~

Verse 13

~~Not sharing, or saving too much is harmful~~

Verse 14

~~Be wise where you put your money~~

If you feel as though you've read these verses before, that's because Solomon has struggled with each of these issues before. Reminding us in verse 10 that death is life's only guarantee, he seems to focus on the seekers who never surrender . . . the religious lost. These "wicked" were actually people he observed going in and out of the holy place, yet their lives gave evidence to the fact they didn't really know the Lord. They may have been given a grand funeral with beautiful eulogies, but they will soon be forgotten and it will be evident they lived their lives in vain.

Verse 11 is a commentary on our modern-day judicial system as it explains why our court systems can't keep up with the crime rate. Crimes continue to be committed because people think they can get away with them. There's a revolving door in our justice system and those who carry out such crimes are well aware of it.

Now, we'll turn our attention to verses 12 through 14. Here Solomon gives a picture of a man who is at rest with the knowledge that God is in complete control and that one day all wrongs will be made right. This is a familiar struggle for Solomon (Ecclesiastes 6:12; 7:15; 8:8). He seems to have a very difficult time dealing with the reality that wicked men appear to fare well, while godly men seem to suffer. However, he consoles himself with the understanding there is a day of reckoning. He sees hope in the truth this life is temporary and that one day all things will be rectified for eternity. He found hope and even joy when he brought himself back into the proper perspective . . . the eternal perspective of life.

Remember, the one who lives with an eternal perspective is the one who truly lives.

Remember, the one who lives with an eternal perspective is the one who truly lives.

With that in mind, let's look again at our permission slip to enjoy life. Planet Earth is filled with people who experience some very difficult times. The ability to enjoy life seems to escape those folks. Maybe you've been through something recently that has rocked your world and left you emotionally drained. Life is not easy and the events of this life can harden our faces and our hearts. When life leaves us numb, it's important we begin to find our way back to the ability to enjoy the simple things. That requires the discipline of directing our thoughts on Philippians 4:7–9, which in turn will result in the peace of God. My sister, His peace brings joy . . . unexplainable joy . . . even through the heartaches of this life. If you've been holding on to your pain and you're afraid to let it go, today you have permission to enjoy this life.

I've been ministering to women for more than twenty years and I'm well acquainted with the deluge of circumstances that painfully grip our lives. Each hurting heart is dear to me. Each broken heart breaks my own. God has placed a love in my heart for women of all ages, all shapes, all colors, and all nationalities, and a desire to minister to each of you. Some of you are facing life-altering circumstances and I want you to know that today's lesson is not meant to minimize your reality. But from the depths of my heart, I want you to know that God sees you, He hears your silent cry, He is with you, and He will bring beauty out of this ash heap you're dealing with right now. If laughter is difficult for you now, please begin to put Philippians 4:7–9 into practice today. You will find that before long, God's peace will strengthen you and the ability to enjoy life will once again be yours.

As we close today's lesson, I'd like to give you some life work (not homework). I want you to wake up each morning and go to bed each night saying something like this:

Morning
"Good morning, Lord! Thank You for a new day, thank You for the breath in my lungs and the ability to live for You today! Thank You for dying on the cross for me . . . for saving me . . . for giving me hope . . . and for having a prosperous plan for my life! I love You, Lord, and today I want this life You have given me to be all about You! Help me enjoy how You work it all out. Help me laugh at myself and help me be a blessing to others. Thank You for loving me."

Thank You, Lord, for loving me!

Night
"Good night, Lord! Thank You for today and for the ability You gave me to live for You! Thank You for dying on the cross for me . . . for saving me . . . for giving me hope . . . and for having a prosperous plan for my life! I love You, Lord, and I hope I made this life all about You today! I enjoyed watching You work it all out. I enjoyed laughing at myself and I was blessed by being a blessing to others! Thank You, Lord, for loving me!"

Before you close out today's lesson, please repeat your memory verse to yourself three times. And remember . . . you now have permission to enjoy this life!
"Who among you is wise and understanding? Let him show by his good behavior his deeds in the gentleness of wisdom." James 3:13 (NASB)

MEMORY TIP
Put your memory verse on the back of your cereal box and study it while you are eating breakfast or having a nighttime snack.

Having a Proper Perspective

DAY FOUR

AH, THE GOOD LIFE!

Ecclesiastes 9:1–10

You may remember the popular television show *Lifestyles of the Rich and Famous* with Robin Leach, which aired from the mid-1980s to the mid-90s. Robin would go to the homes of actors, singers, millionaires, and prominent athletes, and, via television, would take us on a grand tour and show us how those folks lived. At the end of the show, he would often say, "Ah, the good life!"

Our affinity for fame and fortune is really nothing new. Since the dawn of mankind we have always sought ways to better our lives . . . to make things more convenient . . . to live like princesses. I recently watched a movie in which the main character only had to say a word in order to turn his shower on or to have his doors open. Quite a costly piece of technology! Kind of like having a genie in a bottle . . . your wish is his command. Ah, the good life!

Many of those on *Lifestyles of the Rich and Famous* were people with a rags-to-riches story, but Solomon's was quite the opposite. He was a man born with the proverbial silver spoon in his mouth. He was a godly and wise king who had it all and then traded much of what he knew to be right and true for a harem of idol-worshipping women. He didn't lose his wealth, he lost something much more valuable—his testimony. In today's lesson, we'll have the benefit of Solomon's rearview-mirror perspective as he shares with us his riches-to-rags story in hopes we will truly understand what it means to live the good life.

Begin by reading Ecclesiastes 9:1–10. Then mark the statement that best completes each sentence.

I feel that I:	I see life as:
____ Agree with Solomon	____ Easy and carefree
____ Disagree with Solomon	____ Difficult but doable
____ Partly agree with Solomon	____ Painful and impossible

I believe Solomon's view of life is:	My view of life is:
____ Pessimistic	____ Pessimistic
____ Optimistic	____ Optimistic
____ Realistic	____ Realistic
____ Fatalistic	____ Fatalistic

Time and time again, Solomon has reminded us of the brevity of life and he begins chapter 9 the same way. His writings seem to indicate he is insistent on being the bearer of bad news. "Life is hard; life is short; and then you die! No one will remember you. Nothing you do really matters." It all seems so pessimistic, doesn't it? His words of encouragement come in the form of *"a live dog is better than a dead lion"!* With that, he takes a moment to remind us that while we are alive we still have a life to live.

While it's true there are no exceptions to the rule when it comes to death, it is equally true our perspective can determine how well we live this life, as well as how we will spend eternity. Perspective is a choice and is very much shaped by where we are spiritually.

Perspective is a choice and is very much shaped by where we are spiritually.

Solomon was wise enough to know that life is uncertain, yet our ability to really enjoy this life is somehow linked to the reality of our own mortality. Solomon reminds us to enjoy life: the simple things like eating, drinking, working, enjoying each moment, living a pure and holy life, finding pleasure in your marriage, and serving others. These simple pleasures in life are more pronounced when we put life and death in their proper perspectives.

We have the privilege of listening to the heart of the wisest man who ever lived as he speaks through the corridors of time and reminds us to stop and smell the roses along the way . . . to enjoy the simple pleasures of this life. Within the context of one verse (verse 8), Solomon reminds us not only to revel in the routine and ordinary circumstances of life, but that there is no substitute for a pure and holy life. Today, we will journey deep into the vastness of Ecclesiastes 9:8 as we find this particular verse rich with meaning as well as application.

Let's begin by looking at how verse 8 is separated into two distinct concepts. The first is, *"Let your clothes be white all the time,"* and the second, *"Let not oil be lacking on your head."* We're going to begin our quest by looking at the concept of purity first, and then at the end of today's lesson we'll dig into the multifaceted biblical use of oil.

The first time we see white linens used in the Bible is in 2 Chronicles 5:12, 13, where we find the temple choir and orchestra wearing fine white linen and playing and singing in unison the beautiful song "He *indeed is good for His lovingkindness is everlasting."* It was then, in that place, that the presence of the Lord was so powerful that a cloud filled the sanctuary and the priests were rendered incapable of continuing their temple duties.

The last time we see white linens mentioned in the Bible is found in Revelation 19:14: *"And the armies which are in heaven, clothed in fine linen, white and clean, were following Him on white horses."* (This refers to us, the children of the Living God!)

Both of these references and most of the references in Scripture relating to white linen signify purity of the believer and further denote joy and festivity. As born-again believers, we have been made clean by the blood of the Lamb. We are positionally pure. Our heavenly Father sees us as pure, because He sees us through the blood of the spotless Lamb of God, Jesus Christ. Oh, how we could park on that precious truth and praise the Living God!

In fact, please just stop now and spend some time praising God. Tell Him how thankful you are that He sees you as pure as He sees His Son.

There is a wonderful peace that comes with knowing our position in Christ, but there is a huge responsibility that accompanies that position. We are to guard our hearts, our minds, and our actions in order to keep ourselves pure. Obviously, it's a lot easier said than done, especially in such a corrupt and impure world. Difficult, yes. Impossible, no. First John 3:3 tells us that the hope we have to one day see the Lord actually prompts us to live pure lives.

There is no pillow so soft as a clear conscience.

There's an old French proverb that says, "There is no pillow so soft as a clear conscience." When we choose to live pure and holy lives, we avoid the guilt, shame, and other consequences associated with impure and unholy living. Unfortunately, many Christians juggle the concept of purity and holiness somewhere between legalism and traditionalism. Our view of what it means to be pure and holy erroneously becomes a list of dos and don'ts, rather than the overflow of being filled with the Spirit and the desire to honor the Living God with our lives.

Living a pure life is an essential element to living the good life. Purity may not be as popular as it once was, but it's still a biblical prerequisite for a blessed life. Matthew 5:8 says, *"Blessed are the pure in heart, for they shall see God."* The promise is the ability to see God . . . not just in the eternal realm of heaven, but as we daily walk with the Lord by faith. Beloved, God calls us to live a pure life, which is a key ingredient in the recipe for living a good life.

The second part of verse 8 says, *". . . and let not oil be lacking on your head."* Oil was a very important part of Jewish life and is mentioned many times in Scripture. It was used in the temple to anoint the priests and the holy things in order to set them apart; it was used in bloodless offerings; and it was used to keep the "pure candlesticks" lit. It was symbolic of power, favor, gladness, and the Holy Spirit. Traditionally, oil was used for a variety of reasons. Look up the following passages and draw a line to the appropriate description of how oil was used.

Psalm 104:15	to cook with
Matthew 25:3, 4	to anoint guests with
Luke 7:44–47	to use at festivities and demonstrate joy
1 Kings 17:12	to soothe skin and make the face shine
Psalm 141:5	to heal
James 5:14	to refer to the Holy Spirit
Psalm 89:20	to make perfume and fragrant incense
1 Samuel 16:13; Acts 10:38	to anoint (set apart) kings

As we have seen, Scripture tells of many uses for oil, but in context, we find that it primarily refers to joyfulness accompanied by the concept of holiness. In Solomon's day, festivities prompted the use of oil as a type of fragrant application expressing exuberant joy and abundance (Psalm 45:7; Isaiah 61:3). In fact, if you were heading out to a party with family and friends, you'd be sure to dab a little bit of this "eau de cologne" on your neck and wrists before you walked out the door.

There is an element of holiness that springs forth from the little word *oil*, and I'd like you to take a little journey with me to find this intricate treasure of truth tucked in Scripture.

"Behold, how good and how pleasant it is For brethren to dwell together in unity! It is like the precious oil upon the head, . . ."

Psalm 133:1,2

📖 Begin by reading Exodus 30:25–31.
Where was the oil to be put and for what purpose?

____

____

____

📖 Now turn to Revelation 1:6; 5:9–19; 1 Thessalonians 4:4; 2 Timothy 2:21; 1 John 2:20, 27.
Explain the connection between these verses and Exodus 30:25–31.

____

____

____

Don't miss this beautiful and prolific correlation, my sister. In the Old Testament, oil was used to anoint the priests, the instruments, and the vessels that were to be set apart and used in service for the Lord. In much the same way, we are anointed by the Holy Spirit when we are saved and birthed into the kingdom of God to be set apart and used in service for the Lord . . . as vessels of honor . . . as kings and priests. What an incredible privilege we have to be set apart and used to honor the Living God with our very lives! Oh, to live our lives as a sweet aroma unto the Lord!

The good life is inherently linked to the constant choice and perpetual pursuit of living a pure and holy life. So today I want to encourage you to take a good look at your life. Are you really enjoying each day? If not, let Solomon's reminder of your own mortality be a catalyst for a new perspective causing you to look at the simple pleasures of life in a whole new way.

Enjoy each day as a gift from God. Eat lunch with some friends; make that call you've been putting off; quit bickering with your spouse over the petty things and start having fun with each other; quit complaining about your job and be thankful you have the ability to work; make a difference wherever you are and wherever you go; but above all—live a pure and holy life. It's the life we are called to live and it's the life that will bring you the most pleasure in all your days, under the sun.

MEMORY VERSE
"Who among you is wise and understanding?
Let him show by his good behavior his deeds in the gentleness of wisdom." James 3:13 (NASB)

MEMORY TIP
Write your verse on a 3x5 card and place it in your Bible.
Say it out loud before and after your quiet time.

Having a Proper Perspective

DAY FIVE

The Inconsistencies of Life

Ecclesiastes 9:11–18

As I began to study for today's lesson, I was compelled to take a trip down memory lane. So I found my high school yearbook and embarked on a journey to find out who was voted Most Likely to Succeed, Best Looking, Most Popular, and Most Athletic. Now, I don't know about your yearbook, but for the most part, my yearbook is a classic tale of how things don't always turn out the way you expect them to. Best Looking, Most Popular, and Most Athletic have unfortunately fallen from their previously coveted titles and are now known as Most Wrinkled from a Tanning Booth, Still Trying to Be Most Popular, and Most in Need of a Gift Certificate to the Gym. Oh, and the verdict is still out on Most Likely to Succeed. Okay, I'm being a little sarcastic, but you know what I mean. We go through life expecting certain outcomes, but life doesn't always turn out as we expect it to, does it?

Sometimes, we just have to play the hand we're dealt.

Many times, we're the ones to blame when things don't turn out as planned, but there are also a myriad of experiences that invade our lives without invitation and put us on an unexpected path. Sometimes, we just have to play the hand we're dealt . . . and, unfortunately, it isn't always the hand we intended to play.

That's what Solomon was writing about in Ecclesiastes 9:11, 12. The New Living Translation puts it this way:

> *"I have observed something else in this world of ours. The fastest runner doesn't always win the race, and the strongest warrior doesn't always win the battle. The wise are often poor, and the skillful are not necessarily wealthy. And those who are educated don't always lead successful lives. It is all decided by chance, by being at the right place at the right time. People can never predict when hard times might come. Like fish in a net or birds in a snare, people are often caught by sudden tragedy."*

We've all seen circumstances like these play out on the stage of life. In our lives, in our friends' lives, and in the lives of others around us. How many times have you heard sentiments such as these? "I was just in the wrong place at the wrong time." Or, "He was just in the right place at the right time."

APPLY In order to personalize this lesson, think about someone whose life took an unexpected turn. Either they were surprised by an unanticipated blessing, or possibly their life took an unforeseen, tragic turn. Please take a moment to describe that event.

No matter how hard we try, we can never be certain that things will turn out according to plan. The best qualified doesn't always get the job; the most intelligent doesn't always get the platform; the hardest worker doesn't always get the promotion; the best speaker doesn't always get the microphone; the best performer doesn't always get the part. It's just the way life rolls sometimes. It's just part of the inconsistencies of life.

We tend to think of those inconsistencies as random, unpredictable, and frequently unfair, but there are also certain comforts that accompany the ironic contradictions of life. You see, if the fastest runner doesn't always win, then snails like me still have a chance. I may not be the most qualified or the most intelligent, but I may somehow squeak through the system and be chosen for the job or get the platform to present my ideas. When I look at my résumé, I'm often reminded why I tend to root for the underdog . . . it's because I am one. Perhaps you are, too. But we are underdogs with a Great Big God who has told us that through Him . . . we can do all things. Therefore, I'm so thankful life doesn't always turn out as expected. If it did, you wouldn't be reading this book right now.

". . . being predestined according to the purpose of Him who works all things according to the counsel of His will,"

Ephesians 1:11

In the New King James Version the last part of verse 11 says, *"But time and chance happen to them all . . ."* The New Living Translation says, *"It's all decided by chance . . . "* In the Hebrew, the word "chance" is *pegà,* and is only used twice in the Scriptures. It means "an event or an occurrence." and must be understood in the proper perspective. In Matthew Henry's Commentary on the Whole Bible we find this very compelling explanation of Ecclesiastes 9:11: "A sovereign Providence breaks men's measures, and blasts their hopes, and teaches them that the way of man is not in himself, but subject to the divine will. We must use means, but not trust to them; if we succeed, we must give God the praise (Ps. 44:3); if we be crossed, we must acquiesce in his will and take our lot." Under the sun, we may call it chance, but there is no such thing to a Sovereign God.

Sometimes, when life throws us a curve ball, our emotions cloud our doctrine and we become confused about the sovereignty of God. It happens to us all. But it is very important we solve the "control" issue from a biblical standpoint.

📖 Look up the following verses and answer the question, "Who's in control?"

Verses	Who's in Control?
Proverbs 16:9, 33	______________________
Proverbs 20:24	______________________
Proverbs 21:1	______________________
Genesis 50:20	______________________

In Ecclesiastes 9:11, Solomon was reminding us we have no guarantees of how things will turn out under the sun, and that we may face difficult times. He even uses the analogies of a fish caught in a net and a bird caught in a trap. Things happen and we have no way of knowing what tomorrow may bring. It's just part of the inconsistencies of living this life, under the sun. In some ways, life's inconsistencies are very comforting; in other ways, they are very disturbing—but they are never a matter of chance.

As we move on to verses 13 through 15, we find Solomon sharing a little story with us. It's the story of a poor, wise man who was able to save a town attacked by a great king and his powerful army. The poor man's wisdom delivered the city from the enemy, but his poverty couldn't deliver him from the city's disregard for him. You see, there is an unfortunate stigma associated with being poor, and no matter how wise someone is, if their wisdom isn't accompanied by an admirable financial status, then respect will tend to be elusive.

Solomon then gives us his final thoughts on the inconsistencies of life in verses 16 through 18 as he declares it's far more important to be wise than to be strong and powerful. A poor man may not be respected and his words may not be heard, but his wisdom is better than a king's foolishness, because wisdom guards against sin. Psalm 111:10 tells us the fear of the Lord is the beginning, the foundation, of wisdom. When we have a proper fear of God, it serves as a constant reminder we will stand before Him one day. That realization helps prevent us from sinning against Him. But one sinner—even a foolish ruler—has the capacity to destroy much good.

That's exactly what happened when Manasseh sinned against God. Manasseh was only twelve years old when he began to reign after his father, Hezekiah, died. The Bible tells us Hezekiah did that which was right in the sight of the Lord, but Manasseh did that which was evil in the sight of the Lord. In fact, not only were his own actions detestable, he also led the children of Israel to do that which was evil.

Our sin oozes into the lives of others.

No man (or woman) is an island. Our lives affect those around us, many times in very profound ways. Our sin oozes into the lives of others. Like a boulder thrown into a small pond, sin has a huge ripple effect.

📖 Please read 2 Kings 21:1–17 and list the many sins Manasseh committed. Circle those of which the people were also guilty.

____

____

____

____

Now that's a long list of sins, isn't it?! Manasseh's wickedness was not limited to his own actions. His sins affected the whole nation and they became guilty of the same iniquities.

Now focus your attention on 2 Kings 21:10–15. Who faced judgment as a result of Manasseh's sin?

____

____

____

What do you think was Manasseh's punishment?

____

____

____

Turn to 2 Kings 24:1–4 and describe the scene of how God's unfolding judgment became Judah's harsh reality?

____

____

____

____

"Surely at the commandment of the LORD this came upon Judah, to remove them from His sight because of the sins of Manasseh, . . ."

2 Kings 24:3

Reading about Manasseh's sinful seductions reminds me of Jesus' warning in Matthew 18:6, where He told the Manassehs of this world it would be better for them to be thrown into the ocean with a millstone tied around their neck than it would be for them to entice someone to sin.

Manasseh's life reminds us of the devastating ripple effect our sin has on others. One person's sin really can destroy much good. Wisdom prevents foolish and sinful behavior. We are wise to listen to the wisdom of others—regardless of their financial or social status.

Under the sun, life is full of inconsistencies. Many times, things just don't turn out the way we think they should. However, we can walk in wisdom throughout this life knowing that whether people listen to us or not, the Living God sees our sincere pursuit of living a life of wisdom that will enable us to avoid sinful behavior and honor Him . . . behavior that will affect us and those in our sphere of influence.

Take a few minutes to meditate on this week's memory verse in light of today's lesson.
"Who among you is wise and understanding? Let him show by his good behavior his deeds in the gentleness of wisdom." James 3:13 (NASB)

Notes

6

Our Heavenly Sieve

Our sixth week ushers in Solomon's final words of wisdom. As he has done throughout Ecclesiastes, he covers the gamut of life experiences, and with crucial counsel he allows us to see his heart. Avail yourself of some final moments at Solomon's feet as he bottom-lines what really matters most in this life we all live, under the sun.

"Let us hear the conclusion of the whole matter: Fear God and keep His commandments, For this is man's all." Ecclesiastes 12:13

DAY 1	**Branded for Life**
DAY 2	**Avoiding Foolishness and Folly**
DAY 3	**Giving, Gravity, and Grit**
DAY 4	**As Time Goes By**
DAY 5	**The Bottom Line**

MEMORY VERSE

"Let us hear the conclusion of the whole matter: Fear God and keep His commandments, For this is man's all." Ecclesiastes 12:13

Our Heavenly Sieve

DAY ONE

BRANDED FOR LIFE

Ecclesiastes 10:1

Today's subject matter is so important and all-encompassing we need to just park on one verse throughout the entire lesson. Today we are going to investigate the power ingrained in the decisions we make, the choices that characterize who we really are, and the indelible impact our lives will have on those around us. Our study today will remind us that one foolish and unfortunate decision has the power to brand us for life and place us on a path marked by shame. It is a topic that warrants more than just a few lines of encouragement because it has eternal implications for each of us and for those in our sphere of influence.

In Nathaniel Hawthorne's famous classic tale, *The Scarlet Letter*, Hester Prynne is hauled into the town square with her infant child, accused of committing adultery and condemned to wear the letter A on her chest as a badge of shame. It was to be a constant reminder to her and all she would come in contact with that she was a sinful woman. One foolish act branded her for life as an adulterous woman and from that time on, everything she did would be in question. She would never again be looked at as a woman of integrity; never again would her opinion be valued; she would never be trusted around another woman's husband; she was forced to wear her shame for the rest of her life. One foolish act . . . a lifetime of consequences . . . an eternity to reflect on those she could have influenced differently.

A godly reputation built over a lifetime can be lost by one single act of foolishness.

Without naming names, we've all known someone with a similar story. One who was once considered godly and then fell into some kind of sin that ruined their ministry and their reputation. Those who were once known to be wise, yet found themselves caught in the same behavior they warned others about, and that one foolish act became an identifying factor in their lives. Maybe that someone is you. That's what Solomon is talking about in today's text.

Please read Ecclesiastes 10:1 and then write it in your own words.

____

____

____

In ancient days, perfume was produced with fragrant herbs and other natural ingredients, and was very rare and expensive, as we learned in Week 4. It was necessary to keep it securely covered to protect it from the flies drawn to its sweet aroma. In verse 1, we are given a vivid picture of how, if we allow certain areas of our lives to go unprotected, we enable the flies of foolish choices to enter in and spoil the aroma of our lives.

Verse 1 reminds us that a godly reputation built over a lifetime can be lost by one single act of foolishness. We are to guard our lives diligently. We are to put barricades around our hearts to prevent us from foolishly falling over temptations. Our lives are to be marked by holiness, not ungodliness. The Bible gives us plenty of examples of those whose lives were marked and marred by one indiscreet, misguided choice.

Take a look at the chart below and fill in the blanks. As you fill in the blank under "Consequences and Who Was Affected," in order to understand the extent of the main character's actions, allow yourself to enter the realm of the emotions of those affected.

Verse	Character(s)	Choice	Consequences and Who Was Affected
Genesis 2:15-17 Genesis 3:6-21			
Genesis 19:15-17 Genesis 19:23-27			
2 Kings 21:1-17 2 Kings 24:1-4 (from last week)			
Mark 6:17-28			

The choices these people made left indelible impressions on those in their sphere of influence. One decision tainted their lives forever. That's exactly what it does to each of us.

The need to guard our hearts and lives against temptation and against the cravings of the flesh cannot be overemphasized. As children of the Living God, we must constantly be aware others are watching us. Those who don't know Christ not only have a certain expectation of what a Christian should act like, but they can also be drawn to or turned away from Christ as a result of our actions. We are ambassadors for Christ (2 Corinthians 5:20). That means He has left us here to represent Him.

". . . we are ambassadors for Christ, as though God were pleading through us . . ."
2 Corinthians 5:20

I would like for you to ask yourselves a series of reflective questions we should all ask ourselves on a consistent basis. Please take the time to really evaluate your life in light of God's Word.

Do you consider yourself an ambassador for the Lord?____________

How does that affect the way you live?

____

____

____

____

Does your life give evidence to others that Jesus loves them? __________

Do you understand that your reputation is valuable? __________

Have you blown your testimony in a big way? ____________

Have you blown your testimony in front of others at all lately? __________

Do you walk in repentance on a consistent basis? ____________

Have you done anything that brings your Christianity into question? _______

Who is watching you?

____

____

____

Do you strive to live in good conscience before God and man? _________

What are some barriers you need to put up to guard yourself from temptation and/or from falling?

____

____

____

____

"Oh, that they had such a heart in them that they would fear Me and always keep all My commandments, . . ."

Deuteronomy 5:29

Our reputations are valuable; they play a huge role in defining us. However, they are also fragile. They can be lost in a moment of time; they can be sold for next to nothing. A damaged testimony has the potential to act like an eraser and wipe away everything good we've ever accomplished. Once we've lost our testimony, we almost always lose a large portion of our effectiveness as well. That's why I felt it necessary to spend the entirety of today's lesson on this subject. All that we are and our potential effectiveness are on the line with each decision we make.

Our lives can exude the beautiful fragrance of being Christ-filled and Christ-honoring, or we can allow ourselves to fall prey to our own fleshly desires or the lures of the wicked one, and stink up our lives. Oh, dear one, I plead with you—guard your heart, guard your mind, make your choices based on your desire to honor God. You will never regret it!

On the other side of today's lesson is the reality that we all blow it to one extent or another. We all need forgiveness and restoration. You see, we may not have to wear a scarlet letter on the lapel of our blouse, but many of God's children are walking around with a scarlet letter on their heart. Perhaps you're one of them. So many Christians trudge through this life wearing their sin on their faces, while their hearts are laden by guilt and shame. We allow ourselves to be bombarded by the guilt for sins that Jesus has already died for and forgiven. Sin has the power to dilute our effectiveness, but the guilt we carry from sin is capable of doing the same.

First John 1:9 gives us the solution to overcoming sin in our lives. Now, I need to take a little doctrinal detour here, because it is important there be no confusion in our understanding of forgiveness. It is paramount we understand that our forgiveness was fully achieved by Jesus on the cross and irrevocably activated the moment we received Christ as our Savior.

That relationship is unchangeable. He (or she) whom the Son sets free is free indeed (John 8:36); He has promised to cast our sins as far as the east is from the west (Psalm 103:12); there is nothing that can separate us from His love (Romans 8:38, 39); He has promised to never leave or forsake us (Hebrews 13:5). We are forever His . . . forever His children, forever His friends, forever His saints, forever His servants . . . forever His. We are forever forgiven.

But, as with any relationship, our attitudes and behavior can cause us to experience a fracture in our fellowship. Since we know that God is holy and cannot sin, if there is ever a time when our fellowship with the Lord is strained, we can be sure it is because of something we need to deal with in our own lives. That's where 1 John 1:9 comes in. It tells us that if we will confess our sins—agree with God about our sins—then He is faithful to forgive us and cleanse us from all unrighteousness.

In the original Greek, the word "cleanse" is *katharizo* and it means "to purify from defilement, to free from guilt and defilement of sins." In other words, my sister, it means that sincere confession of our sins to God will result in not only total restoration of our fellowship with Him, but also complete freedom from even the guilt of our sins. We are wise not to allow the Enemy to weigh us down with the guilt and shame we have been completely relieved of.

Forgiveness is a funny thing. We all need it, yet we find it very difficult to extend to others. In fact, as I was reading Ecclesiastes 10:1, I couldn't help but think about Hester Prynne and her infamous scarlet letter. What if we all had to wear a scarlet letter for our sins? We may not have committed adultery, but what if we had to wear an L for "Lying," or a G for "Gossip" or "Gluttony," or maybe a T for "Temper" or an I for "Impatience"? We're all guilty of sin. There are no exceptions. When the opportunity to forgive others presents itself, we would be wise to quickly forgive because we have been so completely forgiven.

None of us is perfect; we need to give each other room to grow and room to fail. It's important we remember that our willingness to forgive others reflects our thankfulness for our own forgiveness. Don't make someone else wear the scarlet letter of their sin while expecting yours to be readily forgiven. Colossians 3:13 (NLT) tells us, *"Make allowance for each other's faults and forgive the person who offends you. Remember, the Lord forgave you, so you must forgive others."*

We need to give each other room to grow and room to fail.

Now let's get personal. Are you harboring any unforgiveness in your heart? ________

If so, will you stop and meditate on the many sins you have been forgiven of and write a prayer asking the Lord to help you forgive as you have been forgiven?

____

____

____

____

____

Unforgiveness forms weeds of bitterness that take root in your heart and choke out the beauty that truly should be reflected by a child of God. It hurts you so much more than it does the one you're harboring bitterness against.

"Keep your heart with all diligence, For out of it spring the issues of life."
Proverbs 4:23

As I am writing this I'm struck with a sense of urgency to encourage you with everything I have to guard your heart, your life, and your reputation. You have the capacity to influence so many people around you. Don't forget that. Each time you choose to honor Christ instead of falling prey to your own flesh, you are putting a beautiful flower in the vase of your life and defining yourself as a woman of God. Protect yourself, dear one . . . protect yourself. Don't allow the flies of temptation to putrefy your reputation. Stay clean and close to the Lord. I'm praying for you.

Please take the time to write your memory verse on an index card and review it today.
"Let us hear the conclusion of the whole matter: Fear God and keep His commandments, For this is man's all." Ecclesiastes 12:13

Our Heavenly Sieve

DAY TWO

AVOIDING FOOLISHNESS AND FOLLY

Ecclesiastes 10:1–20

Today's lesson is an adventure in unearthing Solomon's "Tidbits of Wisdom" treasure chest as we begin excavating Ecclesiastes 10, verse by verse. Today we will see the proverb writer Solomon with his seemingly random insights and instructions, yet his overall theme settles on the perils of foolishness and folly as he gives us instructions on how to avoid them.

Begin by reading through all of Ecclesiastes 10. Then we'll begin the process of studying it in segments. We've retraced our verse from yesterday's study because I wanted you to see the whole picture. Solomon begins with a vivid picture describing the importance of guarding our reputations.

As we move on to verses 2 and 3, we see the use of the terms "right hand" and "left hand." In the Bible, the right hand is often symbolic of power, salvation, and blessing, while the left hand is traditionally a sign of evil, foolishness, and the lesser blessings.

📖 Look up the examples of the biblical usage of these terms.

Right Hand: Genesis 48:13, 17–20; Psalm 16:8, 11; Psalm 17:7; Matthew 25:34

What are the blessings associated with the right hand?

First born rights. Protection

Left Hand: Genesis 48:14, 17–20; Matthew 25:33, 41
What do you see associated with the left hand?

Lesser than right, cursed

Verse 2 deals more with contrast of character, while verse 3 deals with the revelation of character, serving as a warning that a foolish person's character will be revealed as time passes. Perhaps you've been discouraged by the fame of the foolish and the undeserved esteem for those who lack integrity. It's quite mystifying. But we can be assured there will come a time when their true colors will come shining through and their true character will be revealed. It's inevitable. This warning should serve as a constant reminder to walk in wisdom, in order that we don't prove ourselves to be fools.

"Why is there in the hand of a fool the purchase price of wisdom, Since he has no heart for it?

Proverbs 17:16

Now, let's begin unearthing the truths found in verse 4. Solomon reminds us there are times when those in high places act as foolishly as the next guy. Yet a calm demeanor diffuses irrational behavior—even when it's the irrational behavior of a king.

📖 Consider what Solomon wrote in Proverbs 15:1 and describe a time when you saw this to be true in your own life.

Every day

I know it's hard, but when the Holy Spirit sweetly and gently reminds us of this biblical truth, we are always wise to listen and obey. Joy floods the soul of the obedient. Of that you can be sure.

As we observe Ecclesiastes 10:4–7, we find that verse 4 gives us a gander at the folly of a leader's bad behavior, and verses 5 through 7 allow us to reflect on a leader's bad decisions.

It is very important that those who are placed in positions of authority understand the responsibility that accompanies their position. Frequently, power and position are given to those who lack the integrity and the experience to effectively lead. Unfortunately, the result can potentially cripple a company—or even a country.

📖 Please read over Ecclesiastes 10:8–10, as we find that our excavation takes us to a treasure viewed by theologians in two different lights. One view is that these verses are taken at face value and refer to the dangers associated with hard work, while the second view is based on the folly of the faulty motives behind each possibly symbolic activity.

I tend to see value in both views, so, beginning with the first, I'd like to touch on both. I am blessed to have a husband who can do just about anything. Before we went on the mission field he owned a landscape company and when we returned to the States, he began a home improvement business. He is definitely no stranger to hard work.

"If the ax is dull, And one does not sharpen the edge, Then he must use more strength; But wisdom brings success."
Ecclesiastes 10:10

But even though my husband works hard, he is wise to know there is a way to accomplish a job in the safest manner and with the least degree of effort. He is a firm believer in the old saying, "Work smart, not hard." You see, he understands there are ways to accomplish the job while minimizing the hazards that come with hard work. In verses 8 through 10 we are shown various types of tasks and from the first theological viewpoint, we are advised to work smart . . . not hard.

Our second viewpoint gives us a different picture of these verses. Here we are reminded of the principle of sowing and reaping. The Bible tells us more than once that we will reap what we sow. Dealing more with foolish motives, this perspective conveys the wisdom to understand the consequences we can expect if we foolishly or maliciously try to cut corners or harm someone else.

As I look at these verses from the aspect of the folly of foolish intentions, I can't help but think of Haman. Let's take a look at a few verses that remind us of the biblical principle of reaping and sowing. Then let's look at Haman, a man who exemplified this principle through his own untimely death.

📖 Please turn to Job 4:8 and then to Psalm 7:15, then explain these verses in your own words.

If you plan to do evil to others, it will be done to you. You will do it to yourself. What goes around comes around. Karma

📖 Now look at Psalm 57:6 and explain the folly of the one who fell in the pit.

David's enemies were making a pit for David, but they fell into it instead

📖 Now let's compare Haman's folly with the verses above. Please read Esther 3:2, 8, 9; 5:14; 7:9, 10. Summarize the events that led to Haman's demise.

You see, we must be careful not to manipulate circumstances in such a way that our intent is to harm someone else, physically *or* emotionally. The Bible is clear our motives should be pure and that we are to look out for the needs of others.

📖 Turn to Philippians 2:3, 4 and describe what these verses tell us about our motives.

📖 Now read Hebrews 4:12, 13. If we don't want our impure motives to become the noose with which we hang ourselves, we must carefully filter what we say and do through the sieve of a pure heart.

Solomon continues to help us avoid the pitfalls of foolishness and folly as he reminds us our lips give evidence of our character. I remember that when my children were small, we would sit by the bed every night and work on our memory verses. One of the first verses we learned was Proverbs 29:11: *"A fool uttereth all his mind, but a wise* man *keepeth it in till afterwards."* We learned it from the King James Version and I have always liked the way it reads. It gives us a clear picture of someone who lets her mouth reveal her character by the words she chooses to say or refrain from saying. A wise woman will not spew out every word that comes to her mind but will ponder her thoughts, carefully choosing her words and saying only what is necessary and appropriate.

"Discretion will preserve you; Understanding will keep you,"
Proverbs 2:11

📖 Take a moment to read Proverbs 25:11. Explain what you think this verse means.

The words we choose to say can actually decorate our lives with beauty and grace. Isaiah said the Lord gave him *"the tongue of the learned, that I should know how to speak a word in season to* him that is *weary"* (Isaiah 50:4). Oh, that we may know how to speak the right words at the right time, revealing that we are women of the Most High God!

Let's finish this segment of our study with two more verses that reinforce our need to guard our tongues.

📖 Please read the following verses and paraphrase what they are saying.

Proverbs 18:21

____

____

____

Matthew 12:36

____

____

____

Knowing that our speech reveals our true character and being aware of our ultimate accountability for our every word should be reasons enough to guard every word that comes out of our mouths. Let me paraphrase Proverbs 29:11 for today's lesson: *"A foolish woman spews out everything that comes to her mind . . . but a wise woman will meditate on it first and take the time to think before she speaks."* Oh, that we may be wise women!

Does what I am getting ready to say really need to be heard?

Let me share with you something a very wise woman shared with me. It's a question we should ask ourselves before we ever open our mouths: "Does what I am getting ready to say really need to be heard?" Take these words of wisdom with you, dear one. This little question has kept me out of trouble more than a few times.

As we wrap up today's lesson with Solomon's final discourse on foolishness and folly, we find ourselves in Ecclesiastes 10:15-20. The foolish king is no better than a foolish citizen. Both live random lives, without discipline, direction or destination. One is the nemesis of his home, the other is the nemesis of a nation.

Solomon's final admonition reverts back to guarding our tongues . . . especially regarding the king. Even if a ruler foolishly causes his kingdom to come to ruins, the Bible reminds us we are to be careful what we say—or even think—about a ruler. In our democratic society, we may not be familiar with the role of a king, but make no mistake about it, wicked or not, he is given power over life and death..

Our response to ungodly and unwise leadership is found in Scripture.

📖 Finish today's lesson by looking up the following verses and describe their significance.

Exodus 22:28; Acts 23:5; 1 Timothy 2:1–4

____

____

____

____

____

Today we've had the privilege of unearthing some very useful nuggets of wisdom from Solomon's treasure chest. They've reminded us of some very important truths each of us can put into practice on a daily basis. Please take a moment and write out which nugget of wisdom has the greatest value for your life in your present circumstances, and how you can put it to use.

____

____

____

____

____

MEMORY VERSE
"Let us hear the conclusion of the whole matter: Fear God and keep His commandments, For this is man's all." Ecclesiastes 12:13

MEMORY TIP
Review your memory verse by saying it out loud at least three times.

Our Heavenly Sieve

DAY THREE

Giving, Grit, and Gravity

Ecclesiastes 11

For the past five-plus weeks we have had the privilege of sitting at Solomon's feet and learning from the wisest man who ever lived! Through this study, I've grown to love and appreciate the wisdom found in Ecclesiastes. It has dramatically changed my perspective and strongly encourages me to live life on purpose. My prayer is that you, too, have been challenged and changed by this study, and I hope you have gained a much clearer and more realistic perspective of what matters most in this life—I know I have.

I feel as though we are rounding third base and heading for home, but I'm not sure I'm ready to tag the plate yet. Fortunately, we have a few more areas of life to cover with Solomon before we slide into home. I'm so thankful you have taken this journey with me and I want to encourage you to continue this study until the very end with the same diligence you started with. *Don't start getting short-timer's attitude on me yet!*

Today, we're going to cover several areas. We'll be talking about giving, grit (not grits, for you Southern girls), and gravity. Our study today will afford us the opportunity to appreciate the vivid imagery used by Solomon as he teaches us a little more about this life in his school of wisdom called Ecclesiastes.

Normally, I would have you read today's text from your own Bible, but today, I'd like for us to be on the same biblical page. So, please take a moment and read the New American Standard Version of Ecclesiastes 11 below. After that, we will divide our chapter into three specific areas of study.

> *"1 Cast your bread on the surface of the waters, for you will find it after many days. 2 Divide your portion to seven, or even to eight, for you do not know what misfortune may occur on the earth. 3 If the clouds are full, they pour out rain upon the earth; and whether a tree falls toward the south or*

"He who has pity on the poor lends to the LORD, And He will pay back what he has given."

Proverbs 19:17

toward the north, wherever the tree falls, there it lies. 4 He who watches the wind will not sow and he who looks at the clouds will not reap. 5 Just as you do not know the path of the wind and how bones are formed in the womb of the pregnant woman, so you do not know the activity of God who makes all things. 6 Sow your seed in the morning and do not be idle in the evening, for you do not know whether morning or evening sowing will succeed, or whether both of them alike will be good. 7 The light is pleasant, and it is good for the eyes to see the sun. 8 Indeed, if a man should live many years, let him rejoice in them all, and let him remember the days of darkness, for they will be many. Everything that is to come will be futility. 9 Rejoice, young man, during your childhood, and let your heart be pleasant during the days of young manhood. And follow the impulses of your heart and the desires of your eyes Yet know that God will bring you to judgment for all these things. 10 So, remove grief and anger from your heart and put away pain from your body, because childhood and the prime of life are fleeting."

Giving

Let's begin by looking at the biblical principle of giving, presented in verses 1 through 6. As we review verse 1, we see that Solomon uses cultural imagery as he describes someone throwing seed over the side of a boat into the murky banks of the Nile in expectation of a luscious harvest of grain and rice.

As I studied various commentaries on these particular verses, I found that many well-respected theologians hold two distinctly different views in regard to the meaning of Ecclesiastes 11:1, 2. Since there is plausible merit in both trains of thought, I would like to present each of them, in order to see how profound and practical the Word of God is.

"He who has a generous eye will be blessed, For he gives of his bread to the poor."

Proverbs 22:9

Some believe they refer to the practice of investing, such as a farmer throwing seed over the side of his boat into the marshy soil of the riverbanks in hopes of a bountiful and lucrative harvest. They believe Solomon is advising us to diversify our investment portfolio . . . that is, not put all our eggs in one basket, because we don't know which ones will succeed and which ones will fail. A diversification of our investments will help protect us from total ruin.

However, far more theologians hold to the belief that the rendering of these two verses calls us to a life of giving. Just as the farmer throws seed over the side of a boat in hopes of a bountiful harvest, we, too, are to freely and unselfishly give to those in need, demonstrating that we trust the biblical principle of sowing and reaping to prove itself true.

I've been reflecting on the body of Christ lately and I've been wondering if we are actually being the church God has called us to be. Are we really like the Acts 2 church? Are we really willing to not only recognize the needs of others, but to actually sacrifice in order to meet their needs? Or are we more about getting than we are about giving?

Perhaps we've confused the biblical concept of being blessed by God. We often equate spiritual blessings with material wealth and possessions. In a world where the majority of the people go to bed hungry; in a world where curable diseases take millions of lives in countries without access to health care; in a world where millions more die from the lack of clean drinking water; in a world where persecution is real and tyranny prevents freedom and financial success . . . it seems our focus on material blessings has clouded our view of what some of our real blessings are.

Things like three meals a day and clean drinking water; things like doctors, dentists, and hospitals; things like grocery stores and pharmacies; things like electricity and walls to keep the cool air in and the bugs out; things like cars and gasoline; things like churches and Christian bookstores; things like freedom and opportunity. These are blessings from God . . . for each of us. Oh, sister, we are so blessed!

I'm not saying God doesn't choose to materially or financially bless us. However, if our only validation of God's hand upon us is receiving some kind of tangible "blessing," then we are missing the reality of Scripture and impairing the faith of those who aren't experiencing the same level of wealth.

The church of the Living God is to be known for its desire to help others and its giving to meet the needs of others. Unfortunately, many times we are so consumed with keeping up with the Joneses we don't have anything left to give. Solomon was reminding us that if we are wise, we will be generous givers. May we each throw seeds from a giving heart that will reap a heavenly harvest of blessings and rewards.

"She extends her hand to the poor, Yes, she reaches out her hands to the needy."
Proverbs 31:20

I'd like to show you something very interesting in verse 2. Solomon says we are to *"divide our portion to seven, even to eight."* The words used there point us to *biblical numerology.* Biblical numerology is the study of numbers found in the Bible, assigning significance to the use of these numbers based on their patterns throughout Scripture. With that said, let's look at the numbers 7 and 8 found in Ecclesiastes. The number 7 is the *number of divine completion . . . the perfect, complete, full amount.* So, when Solomon instructs us to divide a portion to *seven, or even to eight,* he is telling us to go above and beyond what is thought to be enough. You may remember Jesus echoed this same principle when He told His disciples to give not only their shirts, but their coats as well; to walk not only the requested mile, but to go above and beyond the expected (Matthew 5:40, 41).

Let's look at the biblical principle of giving and see how we can start implementing it in our lives.

📖 Please read Proverbs 28:27 (NASB) and fill in the blanks.
"He who gives to the poor will lack nothing
but he who shuts his eyes will be cursed."

📖 Please read what Jesus calls us to do in Luke 6:38 (NASB).
"Give, and you will receive.
They will pour into your lap in full.
For by your standard of measure it will be given back."

"They will pour into your lap" comes from the ancient custom of holding out a long robe in order to carry the overflow of grain. The overflow of grain carried in one's robes was like the expected harvest produced in Ecclesiastes 11:1 after the seed was thrown onto the water banks. This is so exciting, dear one, because as the Lord weaves a similar illustration from the Old Testament into the New Testament, He makes His principle of giving very clear.

In 2 Corinthians 8 and 9, Paul addresses the issue of giving as he calls upon the church in Corinth to give to the needs of the church at Jerusalem because they have been affected by a famine in the land.

Please read 2 Corinthians 9:6–8 and answer the following questions:

Verse 6: What is the biblical principle of giving?

you get what you give

Verse 7: What attitude or motive is not to be exhibited when giving to others?

Don't be reluctant or feel preassure

Verse 7: What does God love?

a cheerful giver

Verse 8: God is able to make all grace abound toward us . . . for what purpose?

He will provide us with all we need. We will always hav plenty to share

"But whoever has this world's goods, and sees his brother in need, and shuts up his heart from him, how does the love of God abide in him?"

I John 3:17

Look at the following verses (NASB) and see what God tells us about giving.

Deuteronomy 15:7: *"If there is a poor man with you, one of your brothers, in any of your towns in your land which the* LORD *your God is giving you, you shall not harden your heart, nor close your hand from your poor brother."*

Deuteronomy 15:8: *"But you shall freely open your hand to him, and shall generously lend him sufficient for his need [in] whatever he lacks."*

Deuteronomy 15:10: *"You shall generously give to him, and your heart shall not be grieved when you give to him, because for this thing the* LORD *your God will bless you in all your work and in all your undertakings."*

APPLY Now take a moment to evaluate your life and be brutally honest with yourself as you answer the following questions:

Do you give to meet the needs of others? __________

Are you a cheerful giver? yes

God has called us to be givers . . . to help those in need . . . to cast our bread upon the waters. So, let's get practical and take a few minutes to list those God has placed in your path whom you can bless is some way.

In Ecclesiastes 11:1, 2, we see that Solomon is instructing us to give with two truths in mind. One, we *will* reap what we sow, and two, we must realize that one day the shoe may be on the other foot, and we may be the one with the holes in our shoes in desperate need of someone's generosity.

Solomon continues his lesson on giving in verse 3, using the imagery of clouds so full they burst into rain and shower the earth. We are to give from our abundance and we should give just as liberally as the rain.

Verse 3 goes on to depict a fallen tree. Its fate is final. Wherever it falls, that is where it will lie. It's a picture of death. Once we die, we no longer have the opportunity to give; we will no longer have the ability to impact or influence. Man's character is unchangeable at the time of death. Like a tree that has fallen, once a man's life is over, there is nothing else he can do to change his character, his reputation, or his eternal destiny.

Ecclesiastes 11:4, 5 reminds us that just as we can not understand the way a baby is formed in the womb, we can't understand the effect our gifts may have on others. They may be well received and have a positive impact on someone's life, or they may be unappreciated and squandered selfishly. But we are not called to sit around looking for just the right time, just the right person, and just the right circumstances before we give. We are to give and to give liberally. We are to give graciously, by faith.

". . . He who sows sparingly will also reap sparingly, and he who sows bountifully will also reap bountifully."

2 Corinthians 9:6

Grit

In the 1969 movie *True Grit,* Mattie Ross (played by Kim Darby), hires a U.S. marshal named Rooster J. Cogburn (played by John Wayne) to help her track down her father's killer. The unlikely pair had nothing in common. Mattie was fourteen years old and Rooster was an aging ol' coot with a drinking problem. But they were both scrappy, tenacious, and strong-willed; they both had what was known as "true grit."

Grit is that strength of character that displays itself in courage, commitment, and resolve. Some people have it and some people don't. But it's something we all need.

In Ecclesiastes 11:6, Solomon gives us a his guide to success. We are to be hard workers; we're to be diligent, unyielding, undaunted, and relentless in all we do. Never a quitter, never a slacker, never a sissy. We're to have true grit.

📖 Please read Ephesians 4:28. What are we to do with our hands and why?

Good hard work
Give generousy

Now please read 1 Thessalonians 4:11, 12. What are we called to do in verse 11?

Live quietly. Mind your own business.
Work with your hands

Why (verse 12)?

Non believers will respect the way
we live

Now look at the following verses and describe the contrast Solomon makes between the lazy man and the diligent worker.

Proverbs 10:4, 5; 12:24, 27; Proverbs 13:4
The lazy man

soon poor, harvest disgrace, slave, get little

The diligent man

get rich, leader, makes use of everything they find, prosper

The Bible tells us that whatever we do, we are to do it with all our might and we are to do everything to the glory of God (1 Corinthians 10:31). Working hard, as unto the Lord, not only unto men. We are to be characterized as steadfast, fervent, and faithful, women of determination, women of resolve. We're to have some grit about us. True grit.

At work, we're to be described as one of the hardest-working employees. At home, we should diligently manage our households. In our ministries, others should know we are committed and dependable. Others should know we have our heels dug in and are more than ready to get 'er done. I pray we would all be women with some grit. May we never again be known as wimpy chicks.

Gravity

Solomon closes chapter 11 by giving advice to the young. In Ecclesiastes 11:7–10, he gives us a parallel look at life. On the one side, he says life is sweet . . . enjoy it while you can . . . pursue your dreams and find joy in the moment. Yet, on the other hand, he takes the time to remind them of the gravity of life . . . that when all is said and done, everything they do is ultimately vanity. He takes them on a turbo-tour of the joys of life and quickly directs them to the reality of death as he reminds them to keep the proper perspective of what it truly means to enjoy this life in light of their ultimate fate—the ultimate fate of us all—our accountability before the Living God.

"For we must all appear before the judgment seat of Christ, . . ."

2 Corinthians 5:10

In verse 9, he says, *". . . walk in the ways of your heart, and in the sight of your eyes; But know that for all these God will bring you into judgment."*

Today, we've been reminded it's good to enjoy this life; it's important we give generously; and we are to have some grit about our lives. And while it's fun to have fun, it's imperative we understand the gravity of this life as we view everything we do, every choice we make, through the lens of judgment.

Giving, grit, or gravity. Which area spoke to you today?

____

What are some practical ways you can allow God's Word to change you as a result of today's study?

____

____

____

____

____

MEMORY VERSE
"Let us hear the conclusion of the whole matter: Fear God and keep His commandments, For this is man's all." Ecclesiastes 12:13
How appropriate for today's lesson!

MEMORY TIP
Make your memory verse your screensaver. Every time you sit down at your computer, let it scroll by two or three times before you begin working.

Our Heavenly Sieve

DAY FOUR

AS TIME GOES BY

Ecclesiastes 12:1–8

I had just turned the TV on and was instantly inundated with commercial after commercial about how I can "retain my youthful appearance." It's everywhere we turn. Not only the pressure to look young, but the plethora of products that can help us do just that. In fact, I remember having a conversation not long ago about how easy it is to get caught up in the "staying young" game. My theory on the whole aging process was that it is just the way life rolls. It's part of the process. I had no intentions of falling into the trap of constantly dying my hair and worrying about how to hide the lines on my face. No way—not I. It's all so silly. I was determined to just accept my age and grow old gracefully.

Well, that was at least seven bottles of hair dye and several jars of anti-aging cream ago. My, how time and experience change our perspective! Maybe you can relate?

". . . The desire of our soul is for Your name And for the remembrance of You."
Isaiah 26:8

As we look at today's text, we are reminded that Solomon is speaking from his own experience. Remember, he was writing Ecclesiastes in his later years, so he was well acquainted with the process of aging. Enjoy his use of symbolism as he gives us some advice about living life and growing old.

Because of the colorful wording used by Solomon, I've provided today's verses in the New King James Version. This will lend ease and unity to our study. Please read the verses below and circle each word or phrase you believe is a symbolic expression of aging, and underline the commands found in verses 1 and 6.

1 Remember now your Creator in the days of your youth,
Before the difficult days come,
And the years draw near when you say, "I have no pleasure in them":

2 While the sun and the light, The moon and the stars are not darkened,
And the clouds do not return after the rain;
3 In the day when the keepers of the house tremble,
And the strong men bow down;
When the grinders cease because they are few,
And those that look through the windows grow dim;
4 When the doors are shut in the streets,
And the sound of grinding is low;
When one rises up at the sound of a bird,
And all the daughters of music are brought low.
5 Also they are afraid of height, and of terrors in the way;
When the almond tree blossoms, the grasshopper is a burden,
And desire fails. For man goes to his eternal home,
And the mourners go about the streets.
6 Remember your Creator before the silver cord is loosed,
Or the golden bowl is broken,
Or the pitcher shattered at the fountain,
Or the wheel broken at the well.
7 Then the dust will return to the earth as it was,
And the spirit will return to God who gave it.
8 " Vanity of vanities," says the Preacher,
"All is vanity."

You have to admit, Solomon uses some pretty interesting descriptions for aging, doesn't he? Most of his imageries are actually metaphors for a specific reality related to the aging process. Many of them are expressions of his time, similar to our "Old as the hills" or "The autumn of our lives." But let's face it, growing old ain't for sissies. Age works against you, not for you.

"For of Him and through Him and to Him are all things, to whom be glory forever. Amen."

Romans 11:36

Let's begin by looking at the commands you underlined in verses 1 and 6. They both convey the meaning, "Remember NOW your Creator . . . before your age catches up with you." Solomon begins at the beginning. His command is that we remember NOW our Creator, as he calls us to reflect on the fact we are not random accidents who just popped onto Earth's scene to exist for just a little while and then vanish. God is our Creator. That means each of us was created *by God* and *for God.*

📖 Please read Psalm 100:3 and rewrite it, placing your name in place of "us" and "we."

____

____

____

____

In our quest to find meaning and purpose in this life, it is imperative to the essence of our value to understand we were created by and for a loving God. This truth is an enabling force, giving us clarity in the middle of chaos . . . speaking peace in the midst of adversity and supplying significance to our own existence. It also helps us function to the fullest throughout each stage of life.

May today's study teach the importance of taking advantage of each day. May it stir a desire in each of us to make an eternal difference in the lives of others while we still have life in ourselves. May it cause us to remember, NOW, our Creator.

We're all at different stages of our lives. Some of us are young, some of us are middle-aged, and some of us are in our senior years. So, when Solomon says we are to remember our Creator in the days of our *youth*, you may be thinking your time has already past . . . that Solomon couldn't possibly be talking about you. However, the term "youth" is used to indicate the need to give the Lord our best . . . to serve Him diligently with the firstfruits—the most capable times of our lives—and not wait until time and the effects of age have limited our mind's capability and our body's mobility. So, when we look at "youth" in context with the various results of aging and the progression presented in today's verses, we are quickly reminded of our responsibility to acknowledge the Lord as our Creator, to understand our accountability to Him. No matter the season in which we find ourselves, we must live for Him to the fullest degree our health will allow.

". . . walk circumspectly, not as fools but as wise, redeeming the time, because the days are evil." Ephesians 5:15,16

Unfortunately, many may think this verse implies that their age gives them a license to take it easy and "retire" from serving the Lord. Many feel as though they've lost their ability to relate and, therefore, can no longer be effective. May I remind you that Moses was 80 when God called him to deliver His people from Egypt? Do you know that Joshua was about 60 when he finally led the children of Israel into the Promised Land?

I could go on, but I would like to take a minute to mention a sweet, godly couple who travel from country to country to proclaim the gospel to as many as they can for as long as they can. They're both in their mid-80s. Health may limit you, dear one, but never allow age to do so.

📖 Please read Psalm 92:14 and fill in the blanks.
"They shall ______________ bear fruit in _________ _________; They shall be ______________ and _________________________" (NKJV).

📖 Please read Psalm 71:9, 17, and 18 and rewrite this as a prayer to the Lord.

____

____

____

____

____

____

____

____

____

Look carefully at verse 18 and notice that the psalmist uses the word until. Until he has done what?

____

____

____

Here's my paraphrase: "Lord, don't forsake me when I'm old. Let me continue to be used to declare Your strength to this generation and Your power to the generation to come . . . I'm not done yet, Lord. . . . Please allow me to continue to be a voice crying in the wilderness to as many as I can for as long as I can."

Please listen, dear one . . . the Lord is not through with you yet. This isn't the time to sit back; this is the time to dig in. You and I have a generation to reach! And we are not going to reach anyone from a rocking chair as we casually watch the world go by. Your health may limit you, but don't allow it to stop you. Joni Eareckson Tada is a very inspiring example of how the Lord continues to use us in spite of our physical limitations. We all need to be like Joni, whose life continually echoes, "No quitting allowed!"

"No quitting allowed!"

Before we get into Solomon's elaborate use of the Hebrew language, let's enjoy some humorous expressions of our own:

1. "It may be true that life begins at 50, but everything else starts to wear out, fall out, or spread out."
2. "Three signs of old age: The first is memory loss. I forget what the other two are." (Sir Norman Wisdom)
3. "You know you're getting old when you find yourself in the middle of the staircase and then can't remember if you were going up or down."
4. "Old age is not for sissies." (Bette Davis)
5. "You know you're getting old when you sit in your rocker and can't get it started."
6. "Your secrets are safe with your friends because they can't remember them, either."
7. "You know you're old when a 30-year mortgage seems like a pretty clever scam."
8. "You know you're old when you bite into a steak and your teeth stay."

Let's take a look Solomon's imagery of the aging process. Keep in mind that each description is veiled with the edict to remember our Creator in the days of our youth.

". . . Yet their boast is only labor and sorrow; For it is soon cut off, and we fly away."

Psalm 90:10

Remember your Creator . . .
"while the sun and the light, the moon and the stars are not darkened" – while you can still think clearly, and while you can still act on your creative and brilliant ideas.

Remember your Creator . . .
when the "clouds do not return after the rain"—when you are not bombarded with pain after pain and infirmity after infirmity.

Remember your Creator . . .
before "the keepers of the house tremble"—before your hands and arms begin to tremble.

Remember your Creator . . .
before "the strong men bow down"—your legs, knees, and feet begin to weaken.

Remember your Creator . . .
"before the grinders cease because they are few" —you begin to lose your teeth.

Remember your Creator . . .
before "those that look through the windows grow dim"—your eyesight begins to fail.

Remember your Creator . . .
before "the doors are shut in the streets"—your hearing begins to fade and your speech becomes garbled because you aren't able to open your mouth when you speak.

Remember your Creator . . .
before "the sound of grinding is low"—the ability to chew is lessened due to the loss of teeth.

Remember your Creator . . .
before "one rises at the sound of a bird"—a good night's sleep ends at the crack of dawn . . . when the birds begin to chirp.

Remember your Creator . . .
before "the daughters of music are brought low"—your voice is weakened by the effects of age.

Remember your Creator . . .
before you "are afraid of height and of terrors in the way"—you fear stepping up ladders, stairs, or hills because you are afraid of falling; you are also generally afraid of the unexpected.

Remember your Creator . . .
before "the almond tree blossoms"—your hair turns white like the blossoms of an almond tree.

Remember your Creator . . .
before "the grasshopper is a burden"—you are frail, bowed down, and hunched over like a grasshopper.

Remember your Creator . . .
before "your desire fails"—you lose your sex drive.

Remember your Creator . . .
before "man goes to his eternal home and mourners go about the streets"—your death.

Remember your Creator . . .
"before the silver cord is loosed"—your spinal cord gives way at the time of death;
or *"the golden bowl is broken"*—your brain ceases functioning when you die;
or *"the pitcher* [is] *shattered at the fountain, or the wheel* [is] *broken at the well"*—your heart and circulatory system cease to function.

What a vivid, yet realistic, picture of the aging process! As he has continually done throughout Ecclesiastes, in verse 7 Solomon once again reminds us of our impending death and our ultimate accountability to the Lord.

Then, in verse 8, we see the expression, *"Vanity of vanities, all is vanity"* for the final time. Solomon ends his dissertation on how to live wisely by reminding us that all is vanity. After his very descriptive explanation of the progression of life and our ultimate fate, he reminds us that, unless we

"And as it is appointed for men to die once, but after this the judgment,"
Hebrews 9:27

REMEMBER OUR CREATOR in all we do . . . all we do will be done in vain . . . like grasping at the wind.

It has been said the sum of all fears is that we will live our lives and then come to the end of our days and discover that it was pointless . . . that it meant nothing. It is even worse to know that your life had meaning, but you never really discovered what it was

Take a moment to reflect on your life. Allow yourself the sobering reality of remembering the time you have wasted. Think about the day when your silver cord will be loosed, when your golden bowl will be broken, when your pitcher will be shattered at the fountain and your wheel broken at the well.

What have you done that will matter at that point?

____

____

____

____

____

____

What have you done that will matter at that point?

What do you still desire to do that will actually matter most when your dust returns to the earth?

____

____

____

____

____

____

____

What is stopping you from living this life on purpose? What can you do today to begin your journey of living a life that will not be lived in vain?

____

____

____

____

____

____

____

____

____

____

____

WHAT ARE YOU WAITING FOR? GET BUSY LIVING THIS LIFE ON PURPOSE . . . FOR HIS GLORY . . . MAKING AN ETERNAL DIFFERENCE IN THE LIVES OF OTHERS.

MEMORY VERSE
"Let us hear the conclusion of the whole matter: Fear God and keep His commandments, For this is man's all." Ecclesiastes 12:13

Our Heavenly Sieve

DAY FIVE

THE BOTTOM LINE

Ecclesiastes 12:9–14

Here we are at the end of our journey through Ecclesiastes and I have to admit, it's bittersweet. You have walked with me through the pages of wisdom and I am so honored you have allowed me to serve you in the Word. I so desperately desire that we have not taken this journey in vain . . . that we will not allow ourselves to live another moment in vain, but that we will truly understand what matters most in this life we all live, under the sun. I don't want to spend another day grasping at the wind. I'm certain you don't, either.

Our heavenly Father has armed us with the tools necessary to sift out the essential from the nonessential in light of eternity. I desperately pray that our perspectives have been dramatically changed to see life with new eyes . . . that in the grander scheme of things, our feathers would no longer be ruffled when our car breaks down—it may mean we have the opportunity to witness or minister to the mechanic. That we would no longer be bothered by long lines, rude people, or inconvenient delays—we see through the eyes of God's love and God's perspective and are instantly reminded we can use that occasion to make an eternal difference in someone else's life. When we see the injustices of life or are tempted by this "all-about-me," materialistic world, we will remember that this life is not all there is . . . that there really is an eternity out there where God calls us to join Him. That we would no longer find ourselves languishing in despair and depression over the hardships of this life, but would choose to allow our lives to be a reflection of God's miraculous grace in the midst of our stormy and uncertain circumstances. May we rejoice in each day and each blessing He has given us, and when we see those in need may we be instruments of God's mercy. May He be glorified in all we do and in all we say. May we live this life for so much more than a vapor. *Oh, let it be so, Lord, let it be so!*

Reading today's verses we find Solomon drawing us to his conclusions. He's giving us the bottom line. For me, that's actually a good thing since I tend to be a "bottom line" kind of girl, one who likes things summed up and dished out quickly. On more than one occasion I've been guilty of telling my husband to wrap it up when he was trying to tell me something. With my eyebrow raised and a motion of my hand, I'd just curtly say, "Could you bottom-line it for me?"

Fortunately for us, Solomon wasn't that kind of guy. Ecclesiastes is his detailed attempt to help us understand what matters most. We find ourselves basking in our final moments at Solomon's feet. After covering a vast array of just about every real-life experience imaginable, he bottom-lines what really matters most in this life we all live, under the sun.

Wrapping It Up

Please read Ecclesiastes 12:9–14 and make a mental note of the words *goads* and *nails* found in verse 11 (KJV, NASB, NIV). We'll come back to them later.

Ecclesiastes is not the result of a vacillating man's random thoughts sporadically jotted down with the hopes of conveying some sort of way to make it through this life. It was written by King Solomon, the world's wisest man, the Preacher *(Qoheleth)*. He calls to each of us through the portals of time to listen to his carefully chosen, Holy Spirit-directed words of wisdom.

Solomon was a proficient and well-known writer. (Perhaps being the wisest man to ever live gave him a *slight* advantage over the rest of us.) He wanted us to understand that every word was a labor of love. It may have been he didn't want us to make some of the same mistakes he had. Could it be possible he loved the generations to follow? His motives remain a mystery, but he did give us a look into his heart as he intensely pondered each and every word.

Look at verse 11 in the New King James Version. *"The words of the wise are like goads, and the words of scholars are like driven nails, given by one Shepherd."*
Based on this verse, what are the words of the wise like? goads
What are the words of scholars like?
driven nails

Customarily, a shepherd had several tools of the trade. Two of them were the *goads* and the *nails*. A shepherd would use a goad to prod the sheep in the direction he knew was right and best. The nails extended from the end of a stick of wood used to pull the wandering sheep back and prevent them from drifting too far from the sheepfold and into dangerous territory.

What an appropriate illustration of how God's Word is used in our lives, just like goads and nails, to direct us and protect us . . . True wisdom comes from the Great Shepherd and He has given us His Word in order to direct and protect us, like goads and nails in His loving hands. God's Word is not only powerful, it is profitable and protective.

Take a moment to read two familiar passages and fill in the blanks.

2 Timothy 3:15–17

The Holy Scriptures are able to make you wise for salvation through faith which is Jesus Christ
All Scripture is given by inspiration of Go.
It is profitable for doctrine, for reproof, for correction
That the man of God may be complete, thoroughly equipped for every good work

Hebrews 4:12

The Word of God is living and powerful.
The Word of God is sharper than any two-edged sword.
It cuts or divides what? soul and spirit.
It discerns or exposes what? thoughts and intents of the h

"For if anyone is a hearer of the word and not a doer, he is like a man observing his natural face in a mirror; for he observes himself, goes away, and immediately forgets what kind of man he was."

James 1:23, 24

God's Word is not just another book—*the book you're reading right now* is just another book. God's Word doesn't contain just a few words of wisdom. It is alive. It is life-altering. That's why the passion of my heart is to point you to the Living God and to His Word. You see, it's in your personal time in the Word and in prayer your loving heavenly Father guides you, comforts you, directs you, corrects you, and protects you as He makes His Word jump off the pages of Scripture and into your heart. It is through His written Word (*Logos* in Greek) He speaks specifically to your life . . . to your heart and to your circumstances through what is known as a *Rhema*. I like to call it "A word from *The* Word!"

There's a huge difference between taking the time to read a book and *investing your time* in reading the Word! Books written by man, no matter how wise, unfortunately leave us sifting through each word, determining what is truth and what is error. Solomon says *"much study is a weariness of the flesh"* (Ecclesiastes 12:12 KJV). Don't get me wrong, there is value in reading a variety of books. They are a great source of knowledge and spiritual encouragement—but they are no substitute for the Word of God.

Drum Roll, Please

And the bottom line is . . . *"Fear God and keep His commandments, because this* applies *to every person. For God will bring every act to judgment, everything which is hidden, whether it is good or evil."* That's it? That's the bottom line?

Remember, this is Old Testament stuff here. So is Solomon talking about keeping the myriad of laws doled out in Leviticus and Deuteronomy, or just "the Big Ten"? He doesn't give a long list of dos and don'ts . . . just "fear God and keep His commandments." That's the bottom line.

The expected response to fearing God is that we will keep His commandments because Judgment Day is coming and no one is exempt. We'd like to think our obedience to God is always motivated by our love for Him, but if truth be told, our obedience to God is often coupled with or precipitated by our reverential fear of Him. After all . . . He is God! There is, however, a link between our love for God, our fear of God, and our desire to keep His commandments.

"Do not be wise in your own eyes; Fear the LORD and depart from evil."

Proverbs 3:7

Travel with me to Deuteronomy 10:12, 13 (NASB). Circle each requirement given and underline the accompanying benefit.

> *"Now, Israel, what does the LORD your God require from you, but to fear the LORD your God, to walk in all His ways and love Him, and to serve the LORD your God with all your heart and with all your soul, and to keep the LORD's commandments and His statutes which I am commanding you today for your good?"*

Now read Joshua 22:5 (NASB) and circle the commandments given.

> *"Only be very careful to observe the commandment and the law which Moses the servant of the LORD commanded you, to love the LORD your God and walk in all His ways and keep His commandments and hold fast to Him and serve Him with all your heart and with all your soul."*

📖 Now turn to John 14:15, 21, 23 (NASB) and fill in the blanks.

John 14:15: *If you* love *Me, you will keep My* commandments

John 14:21 (NASB): *"He who has My __________ and __________ them is the one who __________ Me; and he who __________ Me will be loved by My Father, and I will love him and will disclose Myself to him."*

John 14:23 (NASB): *"Jesus answered and said to him, 'If anyone __________ Me, he will __________ My word, and My Father will love him, and We __________ will come to him and make Our home with him.' "*

There is an obvious and fundamental link between fearing God, loving God, and keeping His commands. Take a trip with me for a moment from fearing God to keeping His commands, and I think you'll gain a clearer picture of this captivating connection.

It works like this: Proper, reverential fear enables us to maintain an appropriate perspective of God's holiness. Knowing that God is holy and that we stand in complete and utter ruins before a holy and righteous God gives us the capacity to truly appreciate the depth of His love for us. And when we get a glimpse of His unfathomable love for us—when we actually realize that His love for us was demonstrated by the complete payment for our sin through the sacrificial death of the His Son—we are constrained to love Him in return (1 John 4:19). Our love for God will automatically be displayed by our obedience to Him. Fearing God, loving God, and obeying God are all a natural, and even supernatural, response to knowing Him. Remember, Solomon chose his words very carefully and he intentionally concluded with the solemn reminder of our ultimate fate . . . Judgment Day. It's coming for us all. There are no escape clauses. And although it seems to ominously loom over us, we profit greatly from knowing it is real and unavoidable. Our knowledge of *that* day should provoke us to live *today and every day* fleeing from sin and clinging to the cross. When we live that way, we will not waste another moment grasping at the wind.

Live for eternity. After all, that's what matters most!

Throughout this Bible study, you have read each verse of Ecclesiastes and, in so doing, you have gathered with the assembly at the feet of *Qoheleth* to hear him speak wisdom through the portals of time. God Himself has spoken to us through His Word in order to help us better understand what matters most in this life we all live, under the sun.

As we close the book on our study, I pray we will never close the book on what we've learned. I may have never laid eyes on you, my friend, but God has laid you on my heart. Though our lives may be lived in different places, you have been the object of my thoughts and prayers for quite some time. Do this thing called *life* well, sweet friend. We have a lifetime to make it all count for more than just a vapor—and an eternity to be thankful we did.

Remember, life is short . . . and eternity is long . . . so live for eternity, dear one, live for eternity. After all, that's what matters most!

MEMORY VERSE
"Let us hear the conclusion of the whole matter: Fear God and keep His commandments, For this is man's all." Ecclesiastes 12:13

Works Cited

Week 2, DAY 4 – "Hating Life"

1. http://www.webmd.com/depression/guide/depression-symptoms-and-types

Week 3, DAY 3 – "Take Another Look"

2. *The Lion King*. Produced by Walt Disney Animation Studios in Glendale, California, and Disney-MGM Studios in Orlando, Florida. 1994.

3. *Voice of the Martyrs*. http://www.persecution.com

Week 3, DAY 4 – "You've Got a Friend"

4. By Carole King as performed by James Taylor. © 1971 by Colgems EMI Music (ASCAP). All Rights Reserved.

Week 4, DAY 3 – "Common among Men"

5. Jonathan Clements, *The Wall Street Journal Online*, http://online.wsj.com/article/SB112846380547659946.html

6. A. J. Reb Materi, Finest Quotes, A. J. Reb Materi (n.d.). Finest Quotes.com. Retrieved January 15, 2011, from FinestQuotes.com Web site: http://www.finestquotes.com/author_quotes-author-A. J. Reb Materi-page-0.htm

Week 5, DAY 3 – "Permission to Enjoy Life"

7. John Wesley's *Explanatory Notes on the Whole Bible* as found at Biblestudytools.com, http://www.biblestudytools.com/Commentaries/WesleysExplanatoryNotes/wes.cgi?book=ec&chapter=008

8. Holisticonline.com, http://www.holisticonline.com/Humor_Therapy/humor_therapy_benefits.htm

Notes